SPIRIT QUEST 1969

TRIPPING THROUGH LANDS OF ENCHANTMENT

RONALD J. SCHULZ

Fulton Books, Inc.
Meadville, PA

Published by Fulton Books 2020

ISBN 978-1-64654-171-3 (paperback)
ISBN 978-1-64654-172-0 (digital)

Printed in the United States of America

I see a vision of a great rucksack revolution, thousands or even millions of young Americans wandering around with rucksacks, going up to mountains to pray...
—Jack Kerouac, The Dharma Bums, 1958

We shall not cease from exploration / And the end of all our exploring / Will be to arrive where we started / And know the place for the first time.
—T. S. Eliot

The Author in 1969

To the companions met, loved, and on
their way. We shall meet again.

SPRING 1969: COLORADO ACID CHALLENGE

THE STATE TROOPER THREATENED ME with arrest if I stuck out my thumb again. Hitchhiking—soliciting a ride, he called it—was illegal in Colorado. He radioed my name and description and swore they'd bust me for it, but getting a ride looked doubtful if I didn't thumb it. Traffic slacked off the farther I got from Denver. Plodding along, my arms at my sides, all I could do was crane my neck to smile at oncoming cars.

Sweating in the high noon heat, I trudged south along Route 85. The two-lane highway cut across rolling green and yellow prairie. It was pastureland, sprinkled with small clumps of trees and bushes, and no clear view of the Rockies far to my right. I'd only gotten one short ride and been walking away from Denver all morning. It looked like I'd have to walk most of the way to Trinidad, where fabled Drop City awaited me, but I was in great shape and knew I could handle it. The only thing I dreaded was jail.

Only a few days before I'd dropped out of high school back in Illinois and was on my own, traveling to communes I'd only read about in Time-Life magazines. Finally, my smile paid off and a car pulled over.

"Where to, man?" Two bearded longhairs in beads, tie-dyed shirts, and leather headbands sat in the front seat. The pale, blond driver looked like Jesus. His tan, black-bearded passenger was in a rugged jean jacket. I'd been saved by the right people.

"I'm headed to Drop City," I said as I hopped into the backseat. They looked like they ought to know where it was.

"Far *fucking* out, man," Jesus drawled. "We can only take you as far as Colorado Springs."

"Any mileage is welcome!" My legs needed a rest. The two dudes in front became engaged in some deep conversation that I didn't bother following. Their speech was peppered with words like *groovy, far out,* and they said *wow* a lot. Then the passenger turned to me.

"Here, man. Let me lay a tab of acid on you." He dropped a bright-purple circle onto the palm of my hand before he turned back to his front-seat conversation.

It was the first tab of acid that I'd ever seen, much less held, but at seventeen I was still trying to prove myself and didn't want to proclaim my ignorance. I examined it with care, wondering what to do with this treasure.

The tab was flat, like the wafer you got for communion in church. About two inches in diameter. It was a pretty, delicate thing, divided into four parts by indented lines, like slices of a pie. Should I take it or save it?

I'd smoked my share of grass with minimal results, but acid-LSD I knew only from the negative media coverage. The scare propaganda about messed-up chromosomes worried me, but scientists said there was no evidence for that. Lots of acid-dropping hippies already had what looked like normal kids. Timothy Leary said acid was a gateway into our spiritual depths, a path to self-knowledge. I wanted to explore psychedelics, but later, when I was better prepared for what everyone agreed was a life-changing experience. Fresh out of high school, traveling alone to explore communes I'd only read about, there was enough going on in my life without taking acid miles from a familiar face, but I had nowhere to put it and feared this divine gift could dissolve in the moist warmth of my hand or deteriorate in my pocket. It shouldn't be lost or wasted.

To hell with caution! I downed it whole before I could change my mind. After a few more minutes ticked by, the passenger turned back to me again.

"Hey, man, did you eat it?"

I shook my head affirmatively.

"How much did you take?"

How much? Of course, that's why it was divided into sections.

"I took the whole thing, man."

His jaw dropped, and his eyes popped out like in a cartoon. I'd goofed.

"*Woooow*, man! That was a four-way tab. Heavy shit!" He turned to Jesus. "He ate the *whole* fucking thing, man!"

"Wow!" Jesus shook his head and clucked his tongue.

None of this *wowing* was doing my peace of mind any good. I had to guard my mind from spiraling into panic. No way could I allow these guys to spook me. Fortunately, I was a meditator, a student of the mystic yoga of India and Tibet. Maybe my spirit guides had led me to this challenge, and I was confident I could handle it.

"Hey, man," Jesus called me from my reverie. "Ever take acid before?"

"No, it's the first time."

The passenger reached over the seat and clasped my hand. "Welcome to the Wonderland, brother!"

When they dropped me off, I'd be on my own, like Alice, down the rabbit hole into a strange new land.

THE GUIDING VISION

WE'D JUST MOVED INTO THE still unfinished house in the village of Wood Dale, Illinois, when I was three years old in 1955. As a toddler, I'd been to funerals, which sharpened my curiosity about death. It was, I felt certain, the portal into another reality. I had a hazy recollection of scrambled bits that seemed to be from a previous life. Reincarnation—rebirth back into this world—seemed real and natural to me, although I didn't know that word. Heaven as taught in Sunday school, a final destination after only one life, didn't make sense.

I'd been playing in the yard on a warm summer's day, trying to decide what my next life should be. After a flash of inspiration, I went running out to the back garden, where Dad was busy with a hoe, eager to tell him what I'd decided.

"Daddy, I want to be a soldier in my next life!" Soldiers, I knew, were different from Army men. The latter wore camouflage-green uniforms, whereas soldiers wore blue or red uniforms and tall hats. I'd seen it in comic books and toy advertisements, which resonated with what I assumed were past life memories.

Dad leaned on the hoe, wiped the sweat from his brow, and shouted, "Baloney!" That single word ripped my elation to shreds. I ran back to the front yard, where red-breasted robins cocked their heads, seeming to listen as I laid out my ambitions. Animals would listen to me.

"Dad doesn't believe me, but I *will* be a soldier in my next life, I will!"

Days later my parents put me down in their bedroom for a midday nap, and I drifted into deep sleep. Suddenly I entered what seemed to be wakefulness. There was a deep, melodious sound that vibrated through my being, thrilling every part of my body. Opening my eyes to the ceiling, I beheld a man's face. The rest of his features were vague, but his eyes, stern, kind, and powerful, entranced me. As I stared into them, I felt myself floating up off the bed; the blankets came up with me. The physical sensation was pleasant, although beyond my experience. As I rose higher, the sound and vibration became louder, as if reaching a climactic moment, making me apprehensive, unsure how this experience would end. Would I lose my identity in that being?

Without words, the being seemed to be telling me that I could end this. All I had to do was look away, *if* I really wanted to. Fear overcame my awed curiosity. With all my willpower, I turned my head to the right, where I saw the empty bed below me. Breaking my visual lock on the being's eyes, the vibrating sound ceased. With the spell broken, I dropped, bouncing on the mattress as the blankets landed helter-skelter on top of me. Without looking up at the ceiling, fearful of restarting the experience, I reached around for the scattered blankets, hoisted them over my head, and went back to sleep.

An actual dream followed. Looking for my mother, I wandered alone in a supermarket while a man in a turban, wielding a broad scimitar, chased me. Running for my life, I ducked around aisles of canned goods, evading his slashing cuts by inches. It felt real, although there was an element of slapstick to it. Then I woke up, safe in my parents' familiar bed. The bright, midday sun shone through the slats of the window louvers. I had no doubt that I'd been dreaming the second time. The events before the dream, however, felt too intense to be a mere dream and stayed with me as a subject of reflection.

Without the language to describe it, my parents and grandparents were amused by my childish tale. They humored me, insisting it had come from my overactive imagination, but I knew better. Puzzling over this event, I developed a keen interest in the spiritual or supernatural. Was the mysterious being who raised me up an omnipotent God or some other spirit being? In later years I reproached myself for my lack of courage in turning away from the face and wondered how I would react if it happened again. I wanted to believe

I would not break the spell next time; I must allow myself to be led into whatever mystery awaited me.

To achieve that goal, I would have to master my fear of the supernatural. Why be afraid of our deeper reality? By age five I was attending Sunday school, where they taught me that God the Father loved us enough to sacrifice his only son. They taught me a fun song about how the walls of Jericho, an evil city that had to be punished, came tumbling down after a trumpet blast. All those people within had to be killed by God's chosen people, even the babies and donkeys, as a sacrifice to that jealous God so his people could live in peace in the Promised Land.

According to my teachers, we were weak, sinful creatures, mere sheep that needed to obey a shepherd. That was what God the Father wanted us to be. We must become stupid, helpless sheep, not rational beings who could think for themselves. We were but the sky god's playthings. That stuck in my craw, but I still felt guilty because feeling that way made me a bad Christian, and I'd certainly burn in hell. Going to hell was permanent, my teachers told me, eternal damnation! Only total *belief*, blind acceptance of stupid dogmas, could save us from the Lake of Fire. Desperate to understand the disconnect between a loving god and his hateful jealousy, I devoured the Bible from cover to cover by age ten, discovering how underhanded and murderous my Sunday school heroes were.

Dissatisfied with the Old Testament's glorying in tribal genocide, I reached farther out, devouring all I could find about other approaches to the spirit world, ignoring the danger my elders told me it posed to my immortal soul. I had to see the unvarnished reality for myself.

Fenton High School, Bensenville, Illinois

A WEEK BEFORE GOING TO Colorado I stepped off the school bus and merged with the horde of students filling the halls, but this would not be a regular school day for me. My anguished spirit needed healing. Chucking the burdensome schoolbooks in my locker, I slammed it and skipped out the back door. Forcing myself to a slow walk to avoid suspicion, wary of patrolling teachers, I strolled against the stream of incoming students toward the trees screening the railroad tracks. Fischer's Woods awaited me.

It was a familiar, three-mile hike to my refuge, a little shorter than the trek from my house in Wood Dale. The whoosh of traffic became muffled by trees sprouting new buds as I entered the woodland. Hand over hand I climbed up the fifteen feet to the tree fort, using the notches my friends had cut into the great oak's thick bark long ago. This was the West Enders' hangout. They were the gang I'd been absorbed into since my introduction in eighth grade. Those guys were boon companions, sharing my love of reading and adventure, but they attended Addison Trail School, not my district. I shimmied up the angled braces and swung over onto the platform. Kicking off my shoes, I sat in the lotus posture to meditate. The tensions and petty dramas of high school faded away. Exactly what I needed.

Over the past year it had gotten easier to twist my legs into the full lotus, but after twenty minutes my legs still prickled, and I had to downshift to half lotus. Ever since reading *Tibetan Yoga and Secret Doctrines* by Evens-Wentz and the more basic *Fundamentals of Yoga* by Rammurti Mishra, MD, I'd been exploring the mystic path. Opening to the cosmic reality beyond our shadow world gave me courage and a sense of fulfillment that the dumb blind faith of ortho-dox religion lacked. If I kept at it, I was confident that I would soon open my chakras, climb the stairway to heaven, and access the same spiritual reality that both Jesus and the Buddha discovered. It was a far better route than the one plotted out for me at Fenton High.

School was a factory, churning students into compliant cogs to keep this consumer society and immoral war machine rolling. As a kid my life was in someone else's hands, and I wanted no part of it. We belonged to our parents to mold into copies of themselves, repli-cating the same mistakes they'd made with their own lives, mistakes that had brought us to this critical juncture in history. I'd had more than enough of listening to fools pretending our imperialist cause in Vietnam and Laos was righteous. If we were to build a new and better society, we would first have to bust out of this *follow the leader* straitjacket.

Sitting in the woods, away from the relentless school propa-ganda, I knew what I needed to do. The future laid out for me by a corrupt society was intolerable. To be *me*, I needed to escape my adolescent prison and break out into the real world. Wonderful things were happening out there, where others thought as I did and dropped out to form a new, more caring society. Only a few friends at Fenton thought as I did: the Hickey brothers, Steve Rock, and Dennis Harris. Together we'd put out the only underground news-paper to surface at our school. Despite our timid stance, focusing on the draconian dress code and barely mentioning the draft and Vietnam, the administration came down hard, folding us up like a lawn chair.

Only the Hickey brothers and the West Enders read as much as I. We knew more about current events and international politics than our classmates, but I had more fire in my belly; my raison d'être, I felt, was to be part of the youth revolution. My pals were content to wait a few more years, but I couldn't. I belonged out there, some-where. Every part of my being wanted to join the living history in the larger world. I'd find more friends and adventurous women who were rebels, unlike the bland chicks around here. I longed for a real woman with spirit to be my lover.

Two years ago, at age fifteen, I'd run away to New Orleans, where I survived on my own until a goddamn lying priest betrayed me to the *man*. Recaptured, I'd been brought back to the conformity factory of home and school. Since then I'd done what the authorities demanded of me while continuing to plot against them. It was obvious that we needed a revolution in this country. Reading Marx's *The Communist Manifesto* and Mao's book on guerilla warfare gave me hope and a blueprint for political action. Mao rose from almost certain defeat on the Long March to win against tremendous odds. We too could turn this gigantic American war machine around and save the planet.

On March 26th, I'd turned seventeen. I was six feet tall and lanky. Whenever I asked my parents' permission to quit school, they put me off. *Finish Driver's Ed and get your license first.* Okay, that made sense. Then it was *just finish the semester*. Then, as another one began, it was *just finish the year*. They were playing for time, extracting promises from me one by one, assuming I'd give in eventually, see the error of my ways, and conform. But now it was 1969, my year of destiny, and time was wasting while I sat there and went through the motions of living a life without meaning.

1969 was claimed to be the beginning of an enlightened age, the vaunted Age of Aquarius. All the symbolic or numerological portents were there. Sixty-nine itself was like the yin-yang Tao symbol proclaiming the interdependence of opposites, which harmonized with the sexual image of that number. Male and female engaged in mutual oral sex seemed to be the embodiment of yin-yang. Not that I, still an inexperienced virgin, had experienced it yet. That gave me even more reason to escape my benighted neighborhood for the free love that hippiedom offered. I felt myself destined to be a part of it, but here I was, trapped in high school, being force-fed propaganda that I knew in my heart to be lies.

Invigorated with fresh air and exercise, brimming with fresh confidence, I made up my mind to force the issue and quit school. Walking in the front door, I broached it with Mom. She set down her whiskey-spiked iced tea and flipped out, screaming at me.

You want to what! Drop out of school? I thought we were done with all that crap.

I refused to back down. Seeing my resolve, she finally became sympathetic. She must have realized it was better to let me go with her blessing than have me run away again.

"You'll have to talk to your principal first." Her narrowed eyes bore into me. "Then, if he agrees, you'll have to talk to your father." She shook her head and looked up at the ceiling. "You know as well as I that he won't like it one bit."

Dad and I never had a close relationship, and I dreaded the inevitable shouting confrontation. I blamed it on his German upbringing. His mother was born in Germany, his father a second-generation Kraut. They'd been dead for years and seemed only stern and formal in my fading memory. On Dad's side of the family, they were all short. I was already taller than he but slim, whereas he was bulky, his hair still black and curly. In his old Navy pictures, set up on the piano, he looked like Tony Curtis, who happened to be Mom's favorite singer. I suppose that's why she fell for him a year before I was born. I took after Mom's side of the family. Her dad, Grandpa Ernie, was six foot three.

As the eldest boy with five younger sisters and few friends on our side of town, I was used to being on my own and thinking for myself. Playing the obedient son, I'd accompanied my family on a two-week vacation the summer before, thereby missing my chance to join the Yippee demonstration at the 1968 Democratic Convention. How could I forgive myself for that? I should have been in Chicago's Grant Park, facing the *pigs* with Abbie Hoffman, chanting *The Whole World Is Watching!* with the rest of my kind. We rebellious kids were the future of America and the world. It was our duty to stand up and be counted.

I'd first come across mention of Drop City while doing research in the school library. A Time-Life book, *The Hippies,* was a collection of articles by different authors about the counterculture that was exploding across the United States. A few color pictures inside showed the Droppers building geodesic domes. Colorado with its mountains seemed the ideal location for a commune. I also learned that communes were springing up in Taos, New Mexico. I'd check those out too. A lot was happening in California, of course, but I was leery of going there. Edgar Cayce, the Sleeping Prophet, said a massive cataclysm would drop that coast into the ocean in 1968 or '69. It could be any day now. He had a good track record of predictions that came true.

DROPPING OUT

ADMINISTRATIVE ASSISTANT MR. WHITLOW HAN-
DLED dropouts. Waiting outside his office, I calmed my mind by
practicing pranayama deep breathing. Finally, the secretary ushered
me in.

"What can I do for you, young man?" It surprised me how cordial Mr. Whitlow sounded in this setting, something I wasn't used to
from authority figures.

"I'm seventeen now and dropping out of school." I took the seat
before his neat, ordered desk. "How do I go about that?"

"Hmmm." He leaned back in his swivel chair, cupped his hands
behind his close-cropped head, and gave me an incredulous smile.
"So you want to quit school, eh? Where will you go? What will you
do? Have you thought about that?"

Of course I had, every single day since I'd been there.

"Do you imagine that you have any skills you can use to make
a living?" He seemed to be sneering at me. These guys had all the
answers but couldn't comprehend anything outside the narrow box of
conformity. "Without a high school diploma, you'll have a hard time
finding a good job. Honestly, what skills do you *think* you have?"

"I've been studying yoga," I told him with false assurance.
"Maybe I could teach it." I couldn't tell him my true intention of
joining the hippies.

"Yoga?" His lips curled into a bemused smirk as he uttered that
word, such an offbeat concept to his mind, which was as square-cor-
nered as his flattop trim.

Staring back at him, I refused to acknowledge his contempt
for what I held sacred. "Yeah, I'll find a job. Hatha yoga is popular
these days." Maybe he thought I wanted to teach in one of those yoga

classes for bourgeois housewives. Good, that could make it seem practical to him and avoid a scrutiny of my plans, which he would never approve of.

Mr. Whitlow seemed to be thinking, *Damn saucy kid.* He sucked in his breath before speaking with an air of resignation. "You see my predicament, Mr. Schulz. I've got a commitment to the citizens of this town. My job depends on pleasing the parents of this community regarding their children. They expect us to impose strict discipline, which means I can't just let students drop out unless they get permission from their folks."

"What if I get their okay?"

"Sure. Have them call me and we can let you withdraw from school." He stood up and ushered me out the door.

That went easier than I expected. The day was Friday, April 25th, my final day of school. There was no emancipation proclamation, just a verbal agreement that he would rubber-stamp whatever my parents said. My next hurdle would be confronting Dad when he got home from work at five thirty that afternoon.

Sitting on the grass by the back patio in full lotus position facing east, my hands in a meditative mudra on my knees, I concentrated on my third eye. Ordinarily, as soon as Dad approached, I'd pull my stiff legs out of their locked position, ending my session abruptly. Dad couldn't be expected to understand what I was doing; there were no words for it in his vocabulary. Today, however, I ignored his approach and didn't budge as he parked the car by the garage on my right. I might as well *let it all hang out.* As he walked past me to the back door, he muttered aloud, "What the heck is this oddball son of mine up to now?"

Fuck it, I could never please him in a million years. In the house I heard Mom's exasperated voice: "He's giving us an ultimatum. He wants to quit school again!" As expected, Dad blew his top.

"Let me tell that knucklehead a thing or two!"

I faced his verbal onslaught with all the steadfastness I'd practiced, but I could never be ready for the screaming monster that was my father. The worst thing he could do was kill me; maybe he would. Biting my tongue until it bled, I let him rage at me, waiting for his steam to blow off. And then, after gulping a deep breath, my voice cracking only a little, I spoke up.

"There is no other way for me, Dad. You talked me into putting this off a year. That's long enough, my mind is made up. Whether you give permission or not, I'm going off on my own." Then I gave him a sanitized version of my actual plans. I couldn't tell him that I intended staying at a hippie commune named Drop City.

Flabbergasted and spent, Dad threw up his hands and walked away. That meant I'd won but in this self-reliant, pull-yourself-up-by-the-bootstraps family, financing this scheme was up to my own devices. I only had about sixty bucks in my possession. The rest of the money I'd earned working at the restaurant two years earlier my parents had stuck in the bank, out of my control, safe for when I came to my senses. But I'd gotten used to privation and living on the cheap. If I hitchhiked, I'd make it last, at least until I found people like me, spiritual brothers and sisters. They'd help me find a way to get by. Not every job required a high school diploma from the propaganda mill.

Friday, April 25th, was my final day of school. As usual, my grandparents came over on Saturday. In my room, a map spread out on my desk, I spun a more detailed story for Grandpa, telling him I was going to look for work near Trinidad, Colorado, the town nearest the acre of dry scrubland where Drop City sat, but I didn't mention that. He moved machinery, monuments, and statues all over the United States and knew most of the medium-sized towns in the country.

"Trinidad? Trinidad is just a one-horse town, Buck." Grandpa still called me Buck. "You'd do better to go find work in Denver."

"Well," I spun a lie, "there's a girl from my class, see? She moved out there."

That made more sense to him; living on a hippie commune would not.

"Don't tell Grandma," he said, slipping a fifty-dollar bill into my hand, the same way he'd given me the sixty months ago, as spending money I never spent. "She don't need to know about this, our secret."

Growing up, he'd taught me that we had to keep secrets from *the women* in our mostly female family. Besides Grandma and their only daughter, my mother, I had five sisters and no brothers. Grandma's sister and her two daughters lived with them, downstairs in their building in Chicago. That left Grandpa, me, and Dad as the only men but I bonded with Grandpa. Dad was more like my boss.

Grandma controlled Grandpa's money. He had to bring his paycheck home before cashing it or she'd throw a fit. She was stingy, doling out his meager allowance for cigarettes and incidentals and banking the rest in the same bank where they'd lost all their savings during the Great Depression. Grandpa managed to earn a few extra bucks on the side that he kept from her. What he gave me must have come from that secret stash.

My grandparents' whole relationship seemed based on a confidential, need-to-know basis. Grandma had her secrets too. "Don't tell your sisters," she'd say, slipping me a large bag of candy. I didn't even like candy all that much, but having promised her, I felt honor-bound to eat it all or give it away to friends rather than my sisters.

Grandpa insisted on driving me across Illinois to Davenport, Iowa, giving me a good send-off to Colorado. I'd take the bus to Denver, where he wanted me to find work, but from there I'd hitchhike down to Trinidad.

Dad fumbled with his camera for a last picture before I vanished into the unknown. Dressed in a rough work shirt and jeans, sturdy leather boots on my feet, a blanket roll slung over my shoulder, I posed in front of the prairie adjoining our backyard. It would be a few years before houses with manicured lawns sprang up beside ours. After snapping the shutter, Dad turned away; his shoulders heaved a little. With a start I realized that my no-nonsense father was crying, becoming more human to me. Despite a tight rein on my own emotions, I couldn't help but feel empathy for him.

Both of these human beings who happened to be my parents had my sympathy. Frozen into the subordinate role that I was, I could do nothing for them by sticking around. To them I would forever remain a mere kid. They couldn't take anything I said seriously.

There was too much at stake for me to change my mind and stay. A bright future beckoned. Unlike the last time I'd ventured away from home, I didn't have much money, not even a backpack, but a canteen full of water gave me an edge over the dry country I expected. Instead of a proper knapsack, I rolled my paltry possessions, consisting of a few changes of clothes, into a couple of Army blankets, tied the ends with a rope, and looped it over my shoulder. That's how Confederate soldiers did it during the Civil War, so it ought to work for me. For my mother's insistence on extra footwear, I looped a pair of gym shoes over my neck and felt as well prepared as I could be for the open road.

Grandma presented me with an enormous package of beef jerky and black licorice. Somehow, I had to fit it into my already bulging bedroll. The impracticality of my blanket roll made itself abundantly clear to me as items kept working their way out, and I had to keep reorganizing and retying the thing. It would have to do for now, my moment had come. Grandma and then Mom hugged me with more emotion than usual; Dad, his eyes still liquid and red, solemnly shook my hand as I slid into Grandpa's tan Buick.

Grandpa and I were alike in some ways, completely different in others. As his only grandson, I was his favorite. Orphaned early, he'd also run away from his strict adoptive parents at fifteen and spent much of his life on the road. Even after he married Grandma, he'd remained a tumbleweed, working jobs that kept him away from home much of the time. No wonder he and Grandma had tension between them. Perhaps they were as estranged as my parents but hid it better. It was hard for me to imagine any of them ever being young kids in love.

Neither of us knew what to say to each other on the long drive. I'd been following the civil rights and the other world events that challenged the social order, but Grandpa found Black Power to be a direct personal threat. He'd even told me I ought to investigate the Ku Klux Klan because *they got something to say.* Although I nursed a soft spot in my heart for him, a cultural divide had materialized between us. In these changing times I couldn't speak my mind with Grandpa, much less my father. The members of my family had become my spiritual enemies. How could I reconcile my own *flesh and blood* with the sure knowledge I had of what was right and needful in these times? How could I explain that I'm no longer their compliant kid but a radical hippie at heart? I said little and nodded agreement while Grandpa spoke on that long morning's ride into the west.

"Look for work in Denver, Buck. Then you can go find your girlfriend in Trinidad. A gal's got no use for a guy who's broke, ya know."

Grandpa had experience with that. Much later I learned that he'd been married before meeting Grandma. He'd just gotten out of the Army in 1923. That is, the Army Disciplinary Barracks in Leavenworth, where he'd served three years for desertion. Then he met Violet, a fifteen-year-old girl in Wichita, Kansas. They tied the knot in the Presbyterian Church, whether she was of legal age or not. Penniless, they lived with her parents. Grandpa had trouble keeping a job; at least that's how Violet's mother put it when she initiated divorce proceedings against him a year later. Grandpa had firsthand experience with how difficult it was keeping on the right side of women in the ups and downs of life.

"Buck, if you ever need money or anything at all, call me, not your folks. They just don't understand how it is like I do."

He asked me again why I was going to that *one-horse town* of Trinidad and wondered why I had to go so far away. Couldn't I pull my life together here in the Chicago area? I smiled, thinking that it was ironic coming from a guy who was always on the road and, like me, had been a runaway at fifteen. He, of all people, should know that I had to break away. We lived in different eras, but somehow, under the skin, we were a lot alike.

At last we drove across the great bridge over the wide Mississippi. He pulled over to the curb in front of the Greyhound bus station, shook my hand as he slipped me another thirty bucks. As I shouldered my blanket roll, he disappeared into the traffic. I wondered if this goodbye would be our last. His health had been failing as emphysema shortened his breath.

ASIANS ON THE PRAIRIE

THE SQUAWK OF BUS ANNOUNCEMENTS was sweet music to me. I settled into a chair in the waiting room and drank in the sights and sounds around me. The last time I'd been in a Greyhound station, I was a fifteen-year-old runaway. Now I was seventeen, legally free and on my own. The thrill of being an autonomous person rather than a disempowered boy swept through me like a shot of adrenaline. My body wanted to move. It was all I could do to sit patiently and wait for my bus to be announced. Whatever could go wrong out there in the big, bad world—robbery, assault, jail, betrayal, death— was worth risking rather than leading a droll, meaningless life back home.

Sitting directly behind the driver, my eyes focused on the view beyond the windshield. Iowa's lush cornfields were so green, they almost hurt my eyes. Crossing its flat expanse took longer than I'd imagined; the bus stopped frequently. At one stop a young Asian man boarded and sat directly behind me. Turning around, I introduced myself and jump-started a conversation. He said he was a college exchange student from Thailand, on his way to meet up with his teacher for a field trip.

He was only the second person from Thailand I'd met. In study hall on the first day of my sophomore year, I'd had the excellent fortune to be seated next to Thira. She only giggled when I spoke to her. I had no idea where she'd come from or even if she spoke English, which was unheard of. That didn't stop me from continuing to whisper to her after the bell rang us to silence. I'd looked forward to getting to know that mysterious girl, but it was not to be. In less than my one happy hour before study hall ended, a teacher came and whisked her away from my table, never to return. Henceforth she was always surrounded by a select group of well-bred honor students, insulating her from proletarian riffraff like me.

I didn't even learn that she was a Thai exchange student until later that year when she performed a full-costume temple dance in the school theater. Her beauty and skill fired my imagination. On stage I saw no trace of the shy girl who'd sat beside me.

This Thai fellow on the bus, however, was not shy. After a minute of craning my neck and shouting over the noise of the bus, he invited himself up beside me.

"What do you think about the US involvement in Vietnam?" I asked him point-blank.

"That's a complicated issue. We are a small country, between the sphere of influence of both the USA and China. We have to play along with more powerful ones, like yours."

"I think the Vietcong are the real heroes," I told him, expecting him to agree. "They are patriots defending their country, first from the French colonialists and now from the American neocolonialists."

The bus driver eyed me malevolently through the rearview mirror. "Keep it down back there, will ya?"

We were both too exuberant to do that. The driver wasn't amused by my unpatriotic sentiments. At the next rest stop, he approached us.

"The two of you will have to move farther back so I can concentrate on driving."

"Yes, sir," I said. There was no point in aggravating him.

The Thai and I covered politics and religion thoroughly, and he applauded my knowledge of Buddhism, which may have gone to my head. In his company the rest of Iowa and much of the dreary expanse of Nebraska melted away. He disembarked to change buses in Omaha. I saw him off and stretched my legs. How quickly we can bond with fellow travelers and how painful is the inevitable separation.

Milling around the bus station, I was surprised to see at least thirty short, slim Asian men, not much older than I, dressed in crisp, green military uniforms. They seemed out of place in the middle of Nebraska. I approached one standing by the glass doors. He was wearing a black beret with patches and emblems on his breast and shoulder that proclaimed him to be a member of the Royal Laotian Army. In halting English, he informed me that he was a trainee attached to the US Army, transferring to another military base. He assured me that it was a good opportunity for him to see more of the world than he otherwise could. After training he would be defending his strategic little country against the Pathet Lao and their Vietcong allies, serving *our* national interest. There had to be some good to come of this cross-pollination of culture and ideas, but I doubted it was the one intended by our national leadership.

Colorado

THE SLOW RETREAT OF DARKNESS before the upcoming sun splashed shades of violet and crimson across the treeless land-scape, the prelude to a magnificent dawn. The bus scattered herds of pronghorn antelope that had gathered to feed along the highway. This morning's vision was well worth losing sleep over.

At long last we rolled into Denver. I shouldered my ill-con-ceived bundle of luggage as best I could and stumbled out of the terminal into a brand-new day. In the distance I saw mountains; the scene elated me as I pondered my next step. It was two hundred miles from Denver to Trinidad. I still had enough money to buy a ticket, but my frugal German upbringing bade me spend cautiously, if at all. Hitchhiking due south to Drop City should be a breeze.

Walking backward from the Denver bus station, I raised my thumb at passing traffic. No luck as the morning traffic snarled around me. It would be better to get out of town for a through ride, so I hoofed it to the southbound highway.

My blanket roll hung like a heavy sausage over my shoulder, coming undone as I walked. Stopping under an overpass, I sat down to rearrange the mess. Grandma had packed me a huge supply of Space Sticks, marketed as the food astronauts ate. It was a soft, can-dy-like, nutritious food and came in a variety of flavors: peanut but-ter, chocolate, and vanilla. Then there were beef sticks, smoked jerky, and bags of black and red licorice bits. I began munching on them as I walked. At least I wouldn't have to buy food for a while. After trekking around some baffling cloverleafs, I came upon a spur of southbound Route 25. Sticking out my thumb, I resumed walking backward.

SHIT! Wouldn't you know it? One of the first cars coming my way was a cop. I swung around to face front and kept walking, hoping the state trooper wouldn't bother me, but it was too late. He sounded a quick blast on his siren as he pulled up behind me on the shoulder. I turned around to face the music.

"Where do you think you're going, young man?" he demanded like the no-nonsense Officer Friday on TV.

"I'm going to my aunt's house in Albuquerque," I lied, but only a little, remembering that I did have an aunt somewhere down there. Maybe he'd go easy on me if my destination was family.

"Well, it's against the law to solicit rides on the public roads of the great State of Colorado." He took off his sunglasses so he could bore into me with his brown eyes. "By rights I should take you in, but I'm going to give you a break, as you're new and just passing through. However, if I ever catch you soliciting a ride again, and I'm up and down this highway regularly, I'll take you in to enjoy the hospitality of a Colorado jail cell."

He radioed my name and description over the radio so any cop who spotted me soliciting a ride could nail me. As compliant as I could be, I insisted that I didn't want any trouble. He began reading me the rules of the road against hitchhiking in Colorado.

"Don't raise your thumb or wave at passing cars. If someone pulls over on his own volition and offers you a ride, that's okay, but you can't ask for it." Then, as if to make it a little easier for me, he offered real advice. "Some of these hitchhikers tie a red bandanna around their arm as an attention-getter so someone knows they'd like a ride."

I had such a bandanna and tied it on as I listened with an appropriately submissive demeanor to everything the man said. Finally done with me, he drove on, leaving me trudging along with my back to the traffic. It was a long walk to Trinidad, but at least I'd avoided jail this early in the game.

The traffic thinned out the farther from Denver I got. I was out in the middle of nowhere. Without raising my thumb but with a wide grin on my face, I'd turn to glance back at the oncoming traffic, hoping to see the damn cops before they were on top of me. If I couldn't overtly solicit rides, at least I could inspire the kindness of strangers to offer me the simple courtesy of a lift.

Time passed as the sun grew hotter. My canteen was already half empty, but at least there weren't any more cops. The bastard had been trying to scare me; maybe patrols weren't that frequent out there. I'd have to be more assertive asking for a ride, or I'd leave my bones to bleach on this road. After checking the horizon for anything that looked like a cop car, I stuck out my thumb.

A delivery van stopped. My first blessed ride on this desolate highway. With a sigh of relief, I jumped in. With his short, black hair and white company uniform, the driver seemed square and straight, a regular working-class guy. He asked where to and I said Trinidad but didn't mention Drop City.

"Why Trinidad?"

"I got friends down there," I told him, stretching the truth. "We want to go hiking into the mountains down there." At some point I intended to climb up to meditate and search for a vision like the Indians did, but of course I didn't tell him that part.

The dude laughed condescendingly. "You want to go up into the mountains? You're not really prepared for that kind of trip! You'll never make it in the jeans you're wearing. That denim material will be cut to shreds in no time on the rough chaparral." As he told me this, his hand slid along my leg and fingered the denim material from my knee to my inner thigh, as if to determine the strength of texture.

"What material should I wear?"

"Leather chaps would be best."

Leather was expensive and I was poor. He kept his hand on my leg and kept rubbing his fingers along the material, closer to my crotch.

"Leather has a nice, *smooth* feel to it." There was no mistaking his intention.

I removed his hand and slid farther over on my side of the cab, but he kept reaching for me while asking if I'd ever *done it* and how did I like *it* and finally if I liked boys better than girls. His modus operandi was already familiar to me, ever since riding with a guy in New Orleans a couple years ago. Again, I brushed his hand off my leg with determined finality, but I didn't care to upset this guy enough to lose the ride.

"Sorry, man, nothing personal, you understand. I'm just not interested in men."

"How do you know if you haven't tried it?"

"It's just not my *thing*, man."

"Hey, I'm giving you a ride. You could show me a little appreciation."

"Sure, I appreciate this ride, thanks, but not at any cost."

I'd been propositioned in big cities, like New Orleans, but never expected it out there in macho, cowboy-ridden Colorado. It seemed out of place amid the wide-open places where the buffalo once roamed. We rode in leaden silence a few minutes longer. Suddenly he pulled over at a gravel intersection, said he had to turn off the highway there, and dropped me off. I was glad to be out, even if it was back on the lonesome road without a prayer.

TRIPPING

"WOW, MAN! YOU TOOK THE whole fucking thing?"

We're back at the beginning. The hippies knew what they were talking about when they told me I was in for one hell of a trip. It had been a rash decision. I was alone on the open road, but it was too late to fret about it. I'd continue as if I knew what I was doing.

For an eternity nothing happened. The guys in front fell back into their subdued conversation, ignoring me, alone with my thoughts. The acid took effect as the minutes ticked by. A deep inner space opened, and I fell in. External space, coming in through my senses, appeared surreal and dreamlike. Events telescoped in or drew out, leaving me unsure of the time elapsing or the distance between objects. As a meditator but a stranger to this altered reality, I tried to keep a part of my mind aloof as an observer, aware that my senses couldn't be trusted in a world of illusion, but each micro-moment seemed pregnant with deep significance. These scruffy young men who'd picked me up seemed to be sacred emissaries of a divine revelation, but I couldn't say where I'd end up.

As we approached Colorado Springs, Jesus, the driver, broke into my reverie. "Do you want us to let you off before we get into town? May be easier to get a ride."

I leaned forward, placing my chin on the back of the front seat to talk to him, and for the first time I saw him from the waist down; the sight made me speechless. While his top half looked masculine, beard and all, from the waist down he was dressed as a woman in a short skirt, sheer nylons, and black high-heel pumps with which he was expertly working the clutch, brake, and gas pedals of this stick-shift car. Was he a cross-dresser or was I hallucinating? Hippies were always trying to blow someone's mind. Far out! He'd succeeded.

31

"Which is it?" Jesus repeated. Distracted, I'd lost my focus. When I didn't answer right away, he added, "In town or out here on the highway?"

Oh yeah, that was the question, but I wasn't sure how to answer.

"We'd better drop him here," his friend whispered. We were still on the outskirts, surrounded by open fields. Maybe they didn't want anyone to see them drop me off, as messed up as I might have seemed. With a cheery "Good luck and be cool, man!" I found my feet back on terra firma, which felt anything but firm. Concrete reality was no longer the solid and dependable thing it had seemed before.

It was early afternoon; I continued walking. US Highway 85-87 became Nevada Avenue, with sidewalks, as it cut through town. Neat, single-family houses with well-trimmed lawns and an occasional church lined both sides of the road. I'd made some seventy miles from Denver, but nobody stopped for me in town.

At an intersection it seemed all I could do to cross safely. *Whoosh!* Cars that had seemed far away suddenly flew by too close. Not being able to trust my spatial perceptions made me apprehensive, almost paranoid. Solid objects had become fluid. They didn't retain their usual shape but shifted in size and appeared to wave or vibrate before my eyes. I was losing touch with the three-dimensional world.

Ordinary noises became louder in my state of heightened perception. My canteen, almost empty of water, went *swish, swoosh* at my side in hypnotic rhythm with every step. My breathing seemed louder too. A faint ringing in my ears, which had always been there, became a roar. Little spaces of time opened within each second. Every moment became chock-full of ideas and insights, all of them competing for attention at the same time, breaking into the main narrative of my experience, impossible for me to follow all of them at once. A thought arose that seemed to be a great insight, but before I could nail it down, it was gone, swallowed up in the torrent of other ideas I could not hold on to.

My internal space held more relevance to me than the minor dramas around me, but then trivial things could become huge irritants to my peace of mind.

"Oh, *wow*, man, did you take the *whole* thing?" Those words haunted me, reverberating over and over in my mind, alarming me. Shit, I had to keep a grip on myself and fight down the jagged waves of panic that followed the blissed-out sensations. I had to keep *cool*, not allow myself to forget that I was walking down the highway alone, a stranger in a very strange land, prey to cops or other evil-minded persons who didn't share my vision. If I didn't keep my wits sharp, I'd be a goner.

Irrational guilt and paranoia came barreling out of the dark shadows of my subconscious, taking turns with a lightheaded euphoria that arose from my more optimistic and better-disciplined nature. I had to keep a lid on all these feelings. My pranayama breathing exercises helped me stay calm in the swirling storm of my mind's eye. I inhaled the clean, sagebrush-scented Colorado air, letting all my anxiety go out with the old air. I would not let the psychic gremlins, like the *Maras* who temped Buddha, overwhelm me.

Glancing around, amazed at what had been ordinary, I wondered how I appeared to others, taking extra care to step high over curbs and cross intersections that shape-shifted before me. I must have seemed out of my head. Insanity beckoned, but I would not let this acid make me crazy.

Crazy? Like in the name of my Indian hero Crazy Horse? Crazy could mean touched by divine genius. What was so crazy about recognizing the irrational forces that banged around inside everyone's head? Acid dissolved my preconceptions and opened doors of insight. I needed to be honest with myself while *tripping*, willing to see what others, those smug people who cannot *see* and who think their world is secure, refused to acknowledge. I had to accept even my bent reality for what it was. Layers of great beauty lay within the ugly. Everything was simultaneously beautiful, ugly, and perfect altogether.

I thought I'd better hole up somewhere until the acid wore off. But where? A park. There must be a park around there somewhere. I could hang out inconspicuously and let these mental and sensory images run their course until I could resume my journey in safety.

Walking along a sidewalk with well-kept lawns and middle-class houses reminded me of Elmhurst, the college town near home, except these streets had an exotic Western and Spanish ring to their names, names like Uinitah. Wasn't that the band of Ute Indians I'd read about? Then came San Raphael, Yampa, and Cachela Poudre before the more prosaic Dale and Monument Streets crossed my path. I was in Middle America again. I wondered how bad the cops were in this town and if they'd roust me like the ever-vigilant Elmhurst cops would. Every time I'd walked through Elmhurst on my way home from Chicago, they stopped and frisked me. I felt like a lost, wandering spirit, searching for enlightenment in this quaint, modern city where I didn't belong. I longed to find sheltering woods to hide in.

A guy came walking toward me. With medium-long, curly black hair and beard, he had to be a hippie and would understand. "Hey, man," I began but fumbled for the right words. "You know, man, I just dropped some acid, see, and like, I never *tripped* before and…"

The sound of my voice seemed alien, like it was another person's words coming out of me, and I wasn't sure how to explain my predicament. With concern flashing on his face, the guy opened his mouth. His white teeth set off by his bushy mustache entranced me as he finished my sentence.

"And you just need a place to hang out until you come down, right?" The words seemed to have deep meaning; he was a mere agent from a higher authority.

I nodded. "Yeah, that's it." I needed to BE somewhere to complete my LSD tutorial, wait until the magic wore off. I needed to merge the metaphysical with my mundane reality, to manifest like a caterpillar into a butterfly, the next stage of my evolution.

He looked pleased with himself at unlocking my dilemma. With a wave of his hand that trailed multiple images of itself, like a multi-limbed Hindu deity, he told me, "Straight ahead, man, only a couple of more blocks." And then the divine emissary went on his way.

Almost there. A few blocks with a loud canteen at my side made it seem to take longer than it should. It created a rushing waterfall in my mind. I reimagined a movie I'd seen about the Amazon jungle.

The green canopy had been brighter than any green I'd ever seen, and the sparking waterfalls seemed inviting.

At last, to my right, was an empty, green park. Safety. The sidewalk branched into a Y, and I angled into it, passing a little placard in cement that proclaimed *Acacia Park*. The letters seemed to vibrate and shimmer. It was a city block square, full of trees and bushes scattered around a well-tended lawn, all of it pulsing with energy.

I flopped beside a bush to enjoy the psychedelic feast unfolding outside and inside of me. Vivid, clashing colors vibrated, dancing before my eyes. Each slat of every ordinary park bench seemed to be painted a different color of the rainbow. The Beatles' song "Strawberry Fields Forever" played in my head. *Nothing is real... nothing to get hung about...* The lyrics seemed written for this experience; each word that popped into my head was imbued with special significance in this, my acid initiation. The outer world reflected what was going on inside my head. The vast universal macrocosm expressed itself in my individual microcosm. My thoughts seemed to come to me from elsewhere, telepathically from a wise being, like my unknown cosmic guru. My spirituality had broken out of the narrow shell of Christian dogmatism years ago to embrace Hinduism and Buddhism. What I'd done in the past over many lifetimes, I thought, had shaped how I saw my current reality.

Therefore, this moment, wandering through strange places on acid, was the exact time and place that I needed to be for my unique destiny to unfold. Each passing event, everyone I saw passing through this kaleidoscope movie of my life, would become a part of my passion play, my cosmic pilgrimage, my individualized stations of the cross. These were not new ideas to me, but they seemed to explode with a visceral force, becoming ever more clear and certain. I had to open myself up to absorb this experience without fear.

The Tibetan Book of the Dead, that ancient tome I'd studied, assured me that I could confront the phantom images of the Bardo, the state between death and rebirth. The same went for dreams, and this experience seemed to be a sort of Bardo dreamland. I must not freak out but, with calm dispassion, allow the mental games to play out before me. Years later I learned that Timothy Leary had written his own book using themes from *The Tibetan Book of the Dead* to guide the acid tripper. In retrospect I realized that I'd been as prepared as I could be for my first journey into the psychedelic Dreamland.

WRESTLING WITH DIVINITY

SACRED WONDERS LAY WITHIN THE most trivial and mundane happenings, things taken for granted, unappreciated until this *now*. Blissful light enhaloed me, seeming to fill my entire body. Was I on the verge of divine illumination? Then I saw that I'd been staring into the sun beating down on me. The sun was bright, and yet a sudden darkness, like a cloud, came over me. Waves of guilt and remorse overwhelmed me as a voice like thunder vibrated in my mind. I didn't so much see as feel the angry sky god. All my life I'd been told that *he* saw everything I did, like Santa Claus. He listed our sins, which were, in truth, our physical needs and spiritual longings, and he lusted to avenge them upon us.

"Thou shalt have no other gods before *me!*" he shrieked, warning me that the *Lord thy God* was a jealous god, a vengeful god. By ingesting LSD I'd polluted myself with offerings to foreign idols and was on the verge of eternal damnation. I'd eaten of the Tree of Knowledge and sinned grievously against the disapproving *God the Father* who watched my every move like a hawk, ready to pounce, willing to destroy that which he and only he had created in the first place.

Christians called him a god of love that must be feared, but he'd revealed himself in the black, leather-bound Bible I'd read as a hateful monster, ordering Joshua and his chosen people to massacre the Canaanites, the people who stood in the way of their possessing the Promised Land. Killing them root and branch. Genocide, that was the price of God's love. His commandments didn't have to make sense; that was the divine mystery. They said I must accept his word without question. *Thus sayeth the* Lord.

Sweat beaded on my body; it ran down my back and to the tip of my nose before it dropped off to nourish the soil of Colorado. I could not escape but must confront *his* wrath. This image of a mad god was but a shade from my Judeo-Christian programming. Frowning preachers who dwelt long on the prohibitions laid out in their ancient black book taught me that *Fear of the Lord* was the height of virtue, the wisdom that was valued most. Their god was a terrorist, demanding we be too humble to rouse the courage to question his orders, but I couldn't oblige, for I'd read that Bible too thoroughly. I'd seen that mad god's naked insanity for what it was and could not accept his totalitarian commandments in good conscience.

I'd long rejected the demonic religion rammed down my throat, yet I still had to face the visceral terror of *what if.* What if this monster, who demanded the genocide of whole nations and the horrific sacrifice of his *only begotten son*, was the only supernatural reality? Was I ready to be steadfast and defy him? Was I ready to be thrown into the lake of fire if I was wrong, ready to burn in hell for all eternity because I could not accept a tyrant for my god?

Death felt close; my youth was no shield. At any moment my body, this collection of arms, legs, a jumping-to-erection penis, and an overactive brain encased in a skull, could become a corpse, a dead thing no longer under my control. My ownership of this body was fleeting, but *something* of my mental-emotional being had to survive physical death. Otherwise, there would be no point in anything I thought or did. How would *I* enter the spirit world, and who, if anyone, would meet me there?

Whether from a chill breeze, or the effect of the drug, or the breath of spirits down my neck, I found myself shaking with an existential terror. Drenched in sweat, I raised my face to the fierce, bright sky. Frowning malevolently from his bejeweled throne, the angry god who resembled my father condemned me before a tribunal of long-faced saints, who then cast their crowns, like lots, into a lake of fire. Since I'd imbibed the forbidden fruit of the tree of knowledge, I'd be damned, *goddamned!* His shrill, angry voice was the voice of my father, my schoolteacher, my pastor. There was nothing I could do to avoid the eternal fires, not if the wacko Christian concept of sin and hell was real. From childhood I'd been trained to obey and fear. No longer! I must strangle that voice, break out of my debilitating cocoon, and escape this hidebound tradition that I'd been raised into.

There was only one refuge: my faith in Buddha nature. I'd take a stand. Like all the bodhisattvas before me, I summoned my courage to defy the Mara-like demon god.

I defy you to your face; you butcher of Canaan and enslaver of the sons of Ham! Whew, I'd gotten that off my chest and felt better for it. I'd told the bogeyman god what I really thought of him, even if he sent me to hell for it. Could he? I waited for the lightning bolt to strike me down. Nothing came.

Feeling stronger, calmer, my conviction grew that the angry god did not exist. Crazy laughter with tears of liberating joy erupted from me as I forced the mental image of the false god, like the wrathful deities of the Bardo, to dissolve. A cool, sacramental blessing of Buddha's accepting love washed through my whole body. Love felt stronger than fear and far more satisfying than dogmatic hatred. This was a great love, the Mahayana all-encompassing, great vehicle love that transcended jealous possessiveness. It bubbled up in me, directed to beings near and far, friends and enemies alike.

MOVING ON

UP TO THAT POINT I'D been alone with the playthings of my mind, then people began filtering into the park. A circle of guys and girls laughed as they scampered around after Frisbees. I overheard comments: *That dude must be tripping, man.*

An older man sat down opposite me, a bum in ragged gray clothing. He began tossing a Wiffle ball, one of those hollow, plastic balls with holes all over it. He asked me, "Wanna play?"

It was a trick ball that bent in flight to pass on the other side of wherever I reached to catch it. Was it me or the ball? Everyone around me clapped and joined in the fun. The bum lit a match and held the flame before me. Its multicolored flames were beautiful, looking less like a real flame and more like something that I could control. I played with it, touching the flame. I felt no pain, only a sort of crumbly sensation as the match head turned to black cardboard ash on my fingers. I wondered if I'd entered a level of Siddhi, psychic power, where fire couldn't harm me. I lit more matches until, finally, I registered the pain. Burned, my fingers felt dry and gritty, as if they, too, were ashes about to disintegrate. Another wave of paranoia assailed me. *Who could I trust from the crowd around me?*

It began to rain. Following the others, I took refuge in the band shell at the back of the park, which was full of a rock-and-roll band's equipment. A blond girl sat above me on a tall speaker beside where I squatted on the floor. She seemed an immense distance above me, and the blue, vaulted ceiling resembled the Sistine Chapel. Gazing up at her, she became angelic, radiating blissful energy from her perch atop a lofty peak. She smiled down at me; her gleaming, white teeth stood out like a Cheshire cat. I tried to talk with her but had trouble getting my voice to work. Its sound seemed to come from elsewhere, each vowel and consonant atomized, echoing in my mind. She laughed, jumped down, and bounced away.

"Hey, man." A long-haired guy squatted beside me. "Are you tripping?" I managed to nod and croak out an affirmative answer.

He looked directly at me, and his eyes bugged out. "Wow, dude, your eyes are super dilated. Where are you from?"

"Chicago." Communication got easier the more I tried.

"No shit? What the hell are you doing here?"

"I'm hitching to Drop City." My answer blew his mind.

"Wow, I heard about that place, never been there."

His friend joined us, smoking cigarettes and then a surreptitious joint, which they shared with me. "Looks like the band's been rained out," he said.

There was a break in the downpour, which would soon continue. They invited me to join them at a restaurant around the corner. I found myself sitting at a table, dry and comfortable, with a group of young students discussing classes and the people they liked and disliked in them. As a stranger on the fringe of their society, I didn't join in the conversation. The food didn't interest me either. Each bite seemed to be composed of small universes, atom-sized planets that made galaxies filled with beings who were having conversations as inane as ours.

I tried drinking the coffee they offered. Its newly strange, otherworldly heat warmed my throat. As I sipped, I watched the unfolding drama of a swirling universe right in my cup.

It was time to move on, but I was unsure about hitching a ride in my tripped-out state. First, I needed to come down from the acid and my inward focus.

"Anyone have a place for me to spend the night?" I asked.

A guy sitting at the next table had an idea.

"There's a Greyhound bus station across from the park."

These good Samaritans led me to the station. With a "Be cool, man," I was on my own, the only customer. Too stoned to organize my thoughts, I felt vulnerable. Before my eyes the timetable of bus departures swirled; I had to focus hard on it. The list of destinations didn't include Trinidad. Maybe it really was a one-horse town, like Grandpa said. Where else should I go? I saw Pueblo and knew it was south but not how close to Trinidad or what kind of town it would be. Gallup, New Mexico was listed. I liked the name; it sounded Western, and I needed the wide-open spaces to clear my head. It was far enough away that I ought to be down from the acid by the time I got there.

The crew-cut fellow behind the counter had been watching me. His eyebrows raised in contempt; he didn't like what he saw of me. My acid goggles exaggerated his expression, making him appear horrible in a comical sort of way, but I knew it was an illusion. Mustering my courage, I dropped my gear on a bench and marched up to the counter. Saying as little as possible, I bought a ticket to Gallup.

A younger worker came in carrying packages from the back. Both men began weighing and stamping them as I sat down on the long, wooden bench to reorganize my gear. Items kept slipping out even as I retied my hopeless bedroll. Tripping on acid made the ropes seem like wriggling worms with minds of their own. All the while, the crew-cut man dropped cruel comments aimed at me.

Even with my still-short hair, he'd pegged me for a hippie. Holding up a string-bound package, he asked his serious-faced partner, "Is this your *bag*, man?" He was mocking the oft-quoted hippie slang term. "Bag" meant somebody's specialty or interest. His partner didn't play along with his barbed joke, and so crew cut had to take both sides of the contrived conversation.

"No, man, *this* is not my *bag*. Is it your *bag*?"

His mocking voice rankled me. Alone on the wooden bench, preoccupied with *my* troublesome bag, I did my best to ignore him while too aware of every innuendo and slur.

A few other people came in and lined up. The bus parked out front, and I clambered in and took a seat with tremendous relief. The neon signs flashed by, and soon we entered the blackness of a rural night. Too keyed up to snooze, I kicked back to let the acid wear off, wondering if it ever would. Could my altered perception be permanent?

Eventually I slept. Bizarre dreams entertained me. Crazy Horse in war paint wrestled in the clouds with a frowning Jehovah, whose beard and flowing white hair became transposed into the face of my clean-cut school principal.

DESERT WALKABOUT

THE MORNING SUN STOOD HIGH over Gallup as I got off the bus, my eyes still unfocused, not sure what was real. Maybe I was still tripping; I had to get my head together. Leaving the bus station, I headed west, passing a succession of cowboy bars, their jukeboxes blaring country tunes into the street even at that early hour. The music lifted my mood. I'd arrived in a genuine frontier town, with chest-high swinging doors on the taverns so familiar to me from Westerns. But I wasn't sure about the attitude of these latter-day cowboys. Rumor had it they hated hippies. My hair wasn't long yet, but it was longer than most of the crew-cut heads hiding under ten-gallon hats that I passed along the street.

Me and my dissatisfied generation, I'd decided, were composed of reincarnated Indians. These cowboys might be our mortal enemies. With my mind still absorbed by such arcane subjects, I didn't trust myself to talk—anything could pop out. I'd have to get my blown mind back together somewhere beyond town. If I'd known an acid trip lasted this long, I'd have saved it for another time.

Beyond Gallup a vista of chaparral and sandy soil opened, and the sweet, intoxicating smell of sage welcomed me as I wandered northwest, the direction that I knew would take me deeper into Native American territory. This was my chance to continue seeking the spirit realm. Turning off the road, skirting human habitations, I headed northwest into the beguiling terrain. As it got dark, I bedded down in a hollow surrounded by brush.

Although I hadn't seen any, snakes worried me. I'd read about the cold-blooded reptiles crawling into someone's bedroll to get warm. It got cooler as the sun set. I lit a small fire for warmth and, I hoped, to keep the snakes away. After it burned down to red embers,

I rolled into my two blankets and curled around the little fire pit I'd scooped out to drift into much-needed sleep. My blankets soon become an entangled mess, and I had to get up and rearrange myself in the dark, causing me to repent not buying a sleeping bag before leaving.

With nothing but water from my refilled canteen to wash down my breakfast of jerky and vanilla and peanut butter Space Sticks, I rolled up my gear and headed deeper into wild country, keeping the rising sun to my back. The Navajo reservation was a huge area, surrounding the Hopi reservation. The Ute, Apache, and several other Pueblo tribal lands adjoined it. Most of the Navajo still lived in hogans, a log cabin-style structure of timbered walls, chinked with mud and roofed over with a hill of earth, giving them a sort of domed top. Many of them had earth piled against the walls, too, for extra insulation. Often there were other wooden sheds or lean-tos nearby for summer use. Sometimes I found a hogan surrounded by clapboard sheds or a modern trailer home and the rusting hulks of cars, the old with the new.

I evaded humans, both Indian and white. I didn't know what social predicament I could walk into. Casting my fate upon the winds, I let the unseen powers, whether gods or blind karmic forces, guide me. I had no idea where I was and only the vaguest notion of where I was going. I wanted a vision, direct contact with spiritual forces like Crazy Horse received after wandering the hills hungry and alone. Fasting seemed vital to that, so I stopped munching my supply of food and prayed, opening my heart to whatever supernatural forces could guide me.

While crossing a dirt track, I passed an old Indian man. He wore a black cowboy hat over his long, white hair, which came out in two tightly bound braids that hung down his chest, almost to his waist. I could have touched him as I passed, but he didn't even look up. He remained squatting on his haunches as if in a deep trance. I wondered if I ought to speak to him or if that would be rude. After I'd passed, I turned back, and only then did he nod, grave and unsmiling, at me. He was the first person I'd met since Gallup and seemed to be in tune with the sacred. I nodded back in reply but, not sure what else to do, moved on across country.

Later I wondered if I should have squatted beside him and started a conversation, intrusive as that seemed at the time. Gliding through another man's country without a proper introduction made me feel out of place, like a phantom, but seeing his acknowledgement boosted my spirits, as if he'd given me his blessing.

After a long day of walking, I watched the daylight fade into the red and purple colors of a vivid sunset. Scraping out a pit, I tended my tiny fire and, with sublime contentment, listened to the whispering wind and occasional night sounds of hooting owls or the yap of a dog or coyote and smelled the sweet-pungent aroma of sage. Feeling quite at home in this wild country, no longer concerned whether the rustling in the brush was a rattlesnake or a harmless rodent, I let sleep overwhelm me.

Early the next morning I turned north on a gravel road. An infinity of scrubland stretched in all directions, and a tumbleweed rolled by. If I saw a car, I'd try to hitch a ride. It didn't look promising, but within the hour, a much-dented pickup truck came into view and pulled over.

In the driver's seat sat a stout young Navajo woman, adorned in blue denim embellished with beads in geometric patterns. A trio of toddlers, crunched in beside her, stared at me with open-mouthed astonishment, as if I were a creature from outer space.

"Where ya *goin*?" Her smile and melodic accent charmed me.

"I don't know," I answered truthfully. Without a map I had no idea and no longer cared.

"Window Rock?" She offered a logical destination.

I nodded affirmatively. "It should be as good a place as any."

"Well, I can take ya down the road a ways." She giggled and gestured at her kids. "But you'll have to ride in back."

Vaulting over the side, I made myself comfortable among burlap bags full of animal feed. The rising sun promised another warm day, although there was still a chill in the air. I hugged myself behind the cab, where less wind caught me as we bounced along at a faster pace than my feet could carry me. In the cab the endearing kids craned their necks to check me out through the back window. I'd been soaking in the majesty of this great land without imposing my expectations on it. Wandering without a destination, homeless, felt like freedom but with a nagging strain of loneliness. It would be nice to share this glory with someone, a brave and confident woman, like this lady seemed to be.

We crossed over a paved highway onto a rutted side road and started to climb a gentle escarpment. She stopped and I jumped out and ran up to the driver's side.

"This is far as I'm goin," she said, but she delayed driving off. Her winning smile and flashing white teeth contrasted with her smooth, nut-brown skin. How nice it would be to give her a hug and a kiss. It had been so long since I'd had a chance at that.

"Where'd ya come from, anyways, to be way out here?"

"Gallup and, uh, before that Chicago." I rambled on about meditation and my spirit quest. She seemed interested, said her father prayed every morning at sunup, but she didn't follow the old ways anymore. Her warm, maternal yet sexy brown eyes met mine. Gazing into them, I felt like I'd jumped into a deep well of refreshing water. This was the first conversation I'd had since leaving Colorado, and I felt drawn to this sparkling woman, even with her passel of kids. I wanted to say something to extend our conversation but was unsure how. With her in my hogan, I'd have no reason to wander alone, lost among strangers as I was.

The fleeting moment passed. With a laugh like tinkling chimes, she put the truck in gear and drove up the bumpy dirt track. The children waved out the back window as they vanished over the rise. Again, I was alone under the vast, blue sky.

Route 264 stretched into the west with an occasional car traveling either way. Another pickup truck came along and stopped.

"*Yah-eh-tehe!*" called a man with long braids in dusty working clothes. "That's how you say *howdy-do* in Navajo. Hop in up front."

The car radio blared the Navajo language on a local station, which surprised me. I was glad to hear a Native American language still in common use and on the radio. Most had become extinct as tribal populations dwindled, but I'd read that the Navajo were growing. Between songs the DJs droned on through commercials made understandable to me by sprinkled English words, like *Ford* and *Chevy* with their corporate jingles. Meanwhile, my host expounded on his culture, fascinating me.

"*Di-ne* is what we Navajo call ourselves. Spaniards called us Navajo, from a Pueblo word, and we called all you people White-Eyes." He laughed at that. "It's because of your lighter-colored eyes, like blue or green."

This jogged my memory to what I'd read on the subject. The Navajo and Apache spoke related languages, and the Navajo Di-ne or N-de name for themselves corresponded to the Apache Tin-de. He spoke of sand paintings used in sacred rituals. They had to be deconstructed and returned to the natural elements afterward, which reminded me of similar Tibetan sand painting rituals I'd read about.

He half turned to me and, with narrowed eyes, asked, "I suppose you heard the stories of medicine men changing themselves into werewolves?"

"Yes, I'd read that in the papers. Any truth to it?"

"There's good and bad sorcery, whether it's magic or using the power of the mind to attack and kill enemies. A genuine spiritual healer wouldn't stoop to it, of course, but if you've got a bad grudge against someone, there's ways to get back at 'em." He hedged on whether he believed a transformation, a two-legged human into a four-legged animal, was possible.

The ride ended too soon as he pulled onto a dirt track, bound for his hogan. I could have chatted with him for hours about the positive and negative use of spiritual energies, a subject that didn't always seem clear-cut. Jesus had cursed a tree that immediately withered and died because he didn't like the fruit. That, among other things in the Bible, smacked of a petty or promiscuous use of divine energy. What if nobody's perfect and even holy people screw up?

With the sun rising overhead, it got warmer. I stuck out my thumb, westward into Arizona. Soon a white station wagon hove into view. A blond white man in his mid-twenties, dressed in slacks and loafers, waved me in beside him and asked me: "Have you ever heard of Mennonites?"

"Yes, my cousin Carol dated a Mennonite." I'd only met him once, but she'd kissed and told me all the fellow's meager secrets before she cast him aside. "Mennonites are related to the Amish, right?"

He laughed as if he was used to Mennonites being regarded as old-fashioned hayseeds. "Not all of us drive around in horse-drawn buggies and wear homespun clothing!"

He said he was a missionary to the Navajo, which put me on my guard, but I kept my response relaxed and casual.

"You see a lot of unique, *err*, interesting people out on the road these days." He smiled and pointed at a spot up ahead. "Right there, last week, I saw another hitchhiker, wearing a long white robe, with long hair and sandals, like Jesus Christ."

"Really?"

"I'd have picked him up if he'd been going my way. Would've liked to talk to him, hear what he had to say about the reason for his get-up. Hitchhikers are usually on the major highways, bound for California, but he, and you, are out here wandering through back roads in Indian country."

Curious about what this missionary really thought about hippies, I questioned him at some length about the times we lived in, the Vietnam War, civil rights, and whether we needed new wineskins for new wine. I told him that I thought the hippie-dropout phenomenon represented a positive transformation of American culture. We could change our consumer-driven society toward an appreciation of the sacred.

"Well," he admitted, "I never really thought about it like that, although I'm a pacifist against all wars."

We discussed his theology, which was straight *believe and be saved* stuff, nothing too deep, mystical, or interesting to me beyond pacifism. Still, he was a pleasant guy, and he invited me to stop off at his home overnight.

"Sure, thanks." I hadn't had an actual meal in several days. My ration of Space Sticks and jerky served me well.

We pulled up to a double-wide trailer overlooking Keams Canyon, which was a small town on the Hopi reservation but surrounded by Navajo. I'd heard about the boundary disputes between the Hopi and Navajo tribes, and my missionary friend confirmed this. Keams Canyon was home to a couple hundred people, with a post office, offices, and single-story houses scattered under the awesome visage of stark cliffs.

Like a cheerful apparition from a Betty Crocker commercial, his pretty, blond housewife and two toddler boys greeted us at the door.

"Are you men hungry? Lunch is ready."

We washed and joined her and the children at the picnic table outside in the shade. The reverend missionary said a long-winded grace before we started in on the typical American meat-and-potatoes meal. Not that I didn't appreciate this fare, but it seemed out of place surrounded by the natural architecture of stratified cliffs and sparse vegetation of the Southwest. We ought to be eating tortillas and beans or venison rather than pork chops and mashed potatoes with wax beans. This blond and blue-eyed family was a patch of suburban Americana set down in the shimmering landscape of a Native American world.

Our polite dinner conversation livened up as I described my trek, but I held back on telling them about my acid experience. Their life centered on raising their boys in Christian certainty and doing *good* as they saw it. Theirs was a mundane, domestic tranquility, a smug happiness which I had to admit appeared charming if not spiritually satisfying. Moreover, I worried about their faith's corrosive effect on Native beliefs and felt duty bound to inquire about them. Although his mission was on their land, he claimed no Hopi as regular parishioners; only Navajo came to services, and he focused his work on them.

"We try to bring the word of God to people in their own language to respect their culture." That, he felt, proved his faith's cultural sensitivity and compassion for their targeted populations. "They are unaware that they were living in darkness. Christ's love," he insisted, "impels us to shine a light into those benighted lives."

While his wife took charge of the kitchen, then readying the children for bed, the missionary and I sat outside in the evening cool. He showed me a large, paperback book entitled *God Bizaad,* which translated as *the Word of God*, the Christian Bible translated into the Navajo Di-ne language. He'd taken a course on the language at the missionary school and claimed that they used the English word *God* because the Navajo didn't have an equivalent word for the supreme creator.

I remembered reading that the Apache and Navajo had a high god named Usen or Yusen. Of course, they had other deities and spirits as well in what I understood to be a rich spiritual tradition. Why hadn't the translators of *God Bizaad* used *Usen* for *God*?

"That would only confuse them," the missionary said. The translators didn't want to put the one *True God* on a par with whatever *pagan* gods the Navajo worshiped. All else but the Judeo-Christian tradition, no matter how profound, was wrong, *pagan* in their eyes.

I began asking pointed questions. "Well, isn't missionary work a sort of cultural imperialism? Don't you think you need to keep an open mind and respect the different culture and traditions of people?"

"Too much of that gets in the way of their salvation. They need a clean break from erroneous beliefs, a mind fresh and open for the Holy Spirit to come in."

Although he had only the best intentions and was kind and generous, his words rankled me. I'd endured enough condemnations from the pulpit. The church's mission, I well knew, was to eradicate, however gently, traditional spirituality. That attitude bespoke arrogance; it didn't seem like true love and respect to me. All my life I'd attended Bible meetings. It always came down to brainwashing and attacking whatever beliefs and opinions didn't fit their totalitarian scheme. Christians claimed all spiritual truth for themselves and bulldozed everything else deep into the subconscious, where it would pop out from time to time, only to be labeled the Devil's seduction. Whatever filled people with awe and gave their lives meaning was the Devil's work.

His wife made up the sofa into a guest bed for me. After a welcome shower I retired to sleep and arose early for a hearty breakfast of eggs, sausage, and pancakes.

CHURCHMEN

THE NEXT DAY BEING SUNDAY, twenty or so Navajo Indians began turning up for the open-air church service, most of them above middle age. Before and after the service, I took the opportunity of talking with them, asking about their original spiritual traditions and what drove them to attend a Christian service. They answered me with good humor. Some admitted to being there on a lark or because a friend had invited them or joking that there wasn't much else to do on a Sunday. Others mentioned a negative personal experience with their own native *witchcraft* or a spat with one of their medicine men. Only a few claimed to be convinced Christians.

What about the Navajo werewolf stories? A wrinkled old fellow who leaned on a cane insisted the stories were true.

"Let me tell you, son," he said, shaking his head for emphasis. "Stranger things than that occur out there in the far canyons. I've seen medicine men do some amazing things. We Navajo have the biggest reservation in the country, and most of us keep to our old ways. I don't mind coming here to pray with these Christians but still see our Navajo healers when I need to."

Everyone agreed the Hopi-Navajo boundary dispute was unfortunate, but as Navajo, their population was expanding faster than the stable Hopi growth rate. They needed more land for grazing their sheep. The Germans called it *Lebensraum*, the need for living space, which has launched innumerable incursions and wars onto other people's land throughout history. Where else are they going to get it? Certainly not from the white ranchers with their entrenched political power.

At the end of his service, which I endured in silence through gritted teeth, my missionary host offered to take me on a drive across the reservation.

"You should meet my Catholic colleague," he told me. "A man more familiar with Native American traditions. He could answer more of your questions." The Catholics, I knew, had first dibs on the territory, dating from early Spanish colonial times.

Waving goodbye to his family, we wound around the canyon, up over an escarpment, and through the desert to an older, more established-looking mission. In a book- and paper-strewn mess of an office, I was introduced to a black-robed Catholic priest who did not seem thrilled at our arrival. Nonplussed, my missionary friend asked him if he could talk to me about the local Indians or find me a place to stay. The priest looked me up and down with cold suspicion without returning my greeting.

I'd learned not to trust priests. Two years before I'd been betrayed by a Catholic priest. He'd turned me in to the juvenile authorities as a runaway at his Skid Row mission in New Orleans, thus ending my first fling with independence. How much difference a couple of years makes. Now that I was seventeen, emancipated and on my own, I had no fears of betrayal.

"Well," he said, drawing it out as if exasperated, "I'm pretty busy these days." He hesitated, gulped, then continued, "I suppose I could take you to some students of Indian culture, if they're still around the reservation."

"That sounds good," the missionary sighed, weary from a long morning of sermonizing and anxious to get back to his family. Their home was cozy enough without me taking up the limited space, but he shook my hand with vigor before he departed. Whatever our differences, he'd seemed to enjoy my visit and conversation.

The priest watched him, stony-eyed, as he left, then said to me, "There've been quite a few young people like you wandering around out here the past few years. I cannot promise anything, they come and go, but I can take you to where I last saw them." He grabbed his keys and led me to the parking lot.

While the priest seemed to take his duty to Mother Church seriously, he must have felt no compunction to waste his valuable time on a strayed hippie. Not when it could be more profitably spent with deserving converts. I felt as if I'd spoiled his limited leisure time and wondered if this was the first time his Protestant colleague had dropped a strayed sheep into his pasture. Then again, maybe I exaggerated what I read into his body language.

HIDDEN VALLEY

THE PRIEST AND I HOPPED into his car and jounced along on rutted, sandy trails that didn't often carry motorized transport. We encountered occasional black-hatted men on horseback or women in long red-and-black dresses that reached the ground. Deeper we drove into the Arizona desert. I enjoyed the scenery that encompassed his rural parish. We passed scattered hogans and flocks of sheep tended by children who waved as we passed. Most of the women and some of the men were kitted out in elaborate turquoise jewelry, festooned about their ears, necks, and waists. At one point we came upon an ancient, wrinkled couple who were hobbling along at the side of the trail. We pulled over, and the priest called out the Navajo greeting, "*Yah-eh-tehe!*"

After a short conversation in Navajo mixed with a few words of English, they squeezed into the back seat, sitting upright and stiff. They seemed uncomfortable and a little afraid as we took off, as if unused to sitting in a car. The man wore a black hat with an eagle feather stuck into the beaded hatband, while the old woman wore a colorful scarf about her head, decorated with elaborate geometric designs. The elderly Navajo were dressed in clean, bright, shining violet shirts adorned with fine turquoise jewelry, as if bound for a gala fandango.

After a few miles the road became smooth. We stopped where the old man indicated. They got out and vanished down another faint track into the underbrush.

After inquiring of several Navajo met along the way, we pulled up to a hogan with a white station wagon parked beside it. Here, seated in a circle with a young Navajo couple, we found three of the young men we'd been searching for. With evident relief the priest left me with them after exchanging a few crisp pleasantries.

Two of them, Pete and Jim, were cheerful, short-haired college students, taking anthropology and social science classes in Santa Fe. The other, Bart, had stringy brown hair in a ponytail down his back. He shared his companions' deep interest in Indian culture and had a deep, personal stake in the matter. A former drifter, he'd come under the spell of the vast country and fallen in love with a local Apache woman. He'd settled into romantic bliss on the reservation.

"You got here just in time," Bart said, rising to his feet. "We're leaving for my place. Want to ride along?"

"Sure, sounds like fun."

"Let's skedaddle then, my honey awaits me! It's called Hidden Valley," Bart said.

I felt darn lucky to have caught them. If I'd missed them, I might have ended up in the company of the dismal priest all night, although I had to admit I owed him for the introduction.

We piled into the white station wagon for another ride through the desert, listening to the haunting tunes of Pink Floyd playing in a loop on their eight-track tape. The music thrilled me as much as our conversation. These guys regaled me with Indian lore and tales of their own thrilling lives.

"Hidden Valley is an amazing place," Bart said. "You'd never find it if you didn't already know where it was. That's where I live now in a funky hogan with my gorgeous woman. She's all I could ever want. Maybe we'll have us a papoose one of these days." He laughed. "You know, I never thought I'd hear myself say that, but guess I'm ready as I'll ever be!"

We rose in elevation, leaving the dry country to enter a forested terrain. Green pines shaded our sun-weary eyes and gave us their refreshing aroma. We finally pulled over at a wide shoulder.

"We'll walk in from here," Bart said. "Look straight ahead and watch your step. You'll be in for a big surprise if you don't."

His warning seemed to be a joke. We crossed a level plain that appeared to stretch out through the pine forest without impediment. But after another step, the ground literally dropped out below us into a steep ravine. We stood inches from the edge of a cliff without any prior indication that it was there.

"See what I mean, man?" Bart crowed, pleased at the dramatic effect his vista presented us. We stood there a moment, taking in the glorious, soul-soothing view. Smoke curled up from the chimney of a picture-perfect hogan down below. With a small vegetable garden and a few flowers nearby, it looked inviting, like a *home sweet home* greeting card.

We wound our way down a steep path to the level bottom. The man of the house ducked inside through the rough wooden door while the rest of us, for decorum's sake, waited outside. The shriek of a feminine voice was followed by a high-pitched greeting.

"Oh, Bart, you're home! I missed you."

That was followed by what sounded, through the door, like bodies slamming together in a rough embrace. It lasted a long moment, complete with lips smacking in lewd reunion, followed by muffled endearments. Then our proud, red-flushed hero popped out.

"Come on in, guys. I want you to meet this fine lady of mine."

She stood close beside him, her black eyes flashing, her long, loose hair hanging to her butt, which was clad in a flowing skirt; a white blouse embroidered with a floral design made a snug fit over her full breasts. No wonder Bart was in love.

"Guys, this is Angelina, the most beautiful woman in Arizona."

She'd been tending the wood fire and cooking, so like Cinderella, her clothing was sprinkled with ash and cornmeal flour, which added to her charm. Her infectious smile, bright as the dawn, put us at ease. She waved us inside, bidding us to be at home, because this, she said forcefully, was *her* hogan! She explained that as an Indian woman, home and hearth were a woman's domain and hers to keep, even if she lost her man. She winked flirtatiously as she said that last part and exchanged a fake-mean look with Bart.

"He's my *old man*," she called her mid-twenties lover, "but he'd goddamn well better measure up, or I'll give him the boot!" She aimed a playful kick at him before he swept her up, laughing as they swirled around the room.

Light came into this windowless womb through the door and via cracks around the smoke hole, through which a jerry-rigged metal chimney protruded. Flames from the stove helped too. A kerosene lantern that hung from a rafter would be lit at night. They spoke of eventually inserting a pane of glass between the logs at one end of the single room dwelling to let in more daylight whenever *he* got around to it.

As water for all purposes had to be carried in from the hand pump outside, they didn't do a full-body wash quite as often as those with running water on tap in a full bathroom. The faint, pungent smell of bodies added a human flavor to the other natural odors from wood, flour, and dried meat.

Angelina asked me if I'd ever seen tortillas being made. I admitted that I hadn't but would love to help. She squeezed off a piece of wetted cornmeal dough and started flopping it between the palms of both hands, patty-cake fashion, until it became flat, round, and thin. She even demonstrated a technique whereby she could flop it with one hand alone.

"Now you try it." She handed me a fresh chunk after slamming her flattened dough right onto the greased top of the potbellied wood stove.

I did my best. My effort, she said, was okay for a beginner as I plopped my poor imitation on the stove next to hers. She flipped them with her fingers when she thought they were done on one side. When we had a plate full, we all dug in, tearing bite-sized pieces off and eating them as is or scooping beans and chili sauce on them. Although the meal was spartan, washed down with sugarless coffee, I found it delicious and filling. I could make do with such simple fare over the long term if I had the satisfaction of this scenery and a fine lady as this beside me.

Jim, the college guy, mentioned that he was going out to meditate in the warmth of the afternoon sun. A great idea. I climbed to a good vantage spot overlooking the valley halfway up the cliff. The smell of juniper and pinion trees mixed with the faint odor of sage and the scent of woodsmoke; it smelled of home. Not my parents' place in Wood Dale but a deep and ancient memory of a home beyond this lifetime, of a past and longed-for future, where I could be at peace with nature and with people who respected and understood me. I was entranced with this Hidden Valley Shangri-La. Life out here felt *real*. Coming from the Midwest, the landscape seemed alien yet alluring. Had I arrived at my destination or was I intruding?

My thoughts bounced from the transcendental to the enchanting land and the bronzed Apache lady, not the way my meditation was supposed to go. Her laughter as she flipped tortillas on her pot-bellied stove, looking with such determined yet warm eyes at her man, impressed me. Maybe I needed to refocus my spirit quest, accept my earthy human limitations, build a firmer base within the physical realm. In short, I needed to find such a woman and settle down out there. With a hot-blooded woman who had the mettle to live a life like this, I'd be fulfilled. We would create a combined new culture to win back our nation from greed and oppression.

The musty tang of human warmth greeted me back inside the dark hogan. I expected to spend the night, maybe a couple of days or even forever, but my collegiate friends needed to return to Gallup and wanted to start before it got dark. They might otherwise get lost on the unmarked tracks that passed for roads. Though I hated to leave, I didn't want to impose on this couple's hospitality. Without a doubt I'd make it back someday.

After hugs and bidding *adios* to our sweet lovers at the door of their hogan, we hiked back up the rise, loaded into the station wagon, and drove away from the secret idyll of Hidden Valley. Back into the dry and desolate Arizona landscape, we continued east to New Mexico. Eventually, we hit blacktop and smoother sailing.

"Gee, I hope we don't run out of gas out here," said Jim. "There's nothing but a long, black ribbon of road ahead of us."

"That won't happen again," said Pete, the driver and owner of the car, grinning with confidence. "I've gotten to know where all the gas stations are." He checked the odometer against a notepad of penciled notes.

Turning to me, he continued, "Ya know, Ron, I've made a science of gauging the number of miles until a fill-up is needed."

But after another twenty minutes, a frown crossed his face. Then he brightened up. "Should be one coming up any minute now."

"Shit," said Jim, indicating the fuel gauge: it was on empty. "It'll be a damn close thing, Pete."

"Nah, there's usually about a gallon left when the gauge reads empty. We'll make it." Then he added softly, "I sure as fuck hope so."

The engine conked out. Pete restarted it but less than a mile later, it conked out again. He popped it in neutral, so we continued to glide as he turned the key. Nothing.

"The gas tank is bone dry, Pete," Jim said. "Lucky we're on a slope."

It was an almost imperceptible downward grade, but Pete hadn't any reason to touch the brake. Leaving it in neutral, we coasted along the empty highway a mile or more.

"There it is up ahead," Pete said, breaking into his usual grin.

Sure enough, just visible up ahead on the left was a gas station. "Think we'll make it, Jim?"

"Sure, we will, just like last time." He turned to me. "Believe it or not, Ron, the same thing happened last time we came this way. Coasting into this station is becoming a tradition."

The slope bottomed out. We slowed down to an agonizing crawl and finally stopped just as we reached the gas station. We jumped out and, with a little extra push across the lane, we made it up to the gas pump as the attendant came out.

"That was even closer than the last time!" said the amazed teen-aged attendant. They seemed to be regular customers.

"We're becoming adept at coasting in on fumes," crowed Jim.

Pete called out, "Fill her up, if you please!" He laughed and added, "You know Jim, we ought to get a big gas can, might come in handy one of these days!"

This episode was the closest-run thing I'd ever seen, but they pretended it was no big deal, just another day in the life of a desert wanderer.

As I got out of the car to stretch with the others, I recognized the station from when I passed through with the Navajo man. It's a big country but a small world when everything comes down to a few watering holes.

We trooped inside. Pete fed some money into a vending machine. Out plopped a silver-sheathed candy bar, branded with the underlined logo *Zero* in bold letters.

"Jeez," I said. "Even the candy bars are different out here."

"You never saw a Zero?" Pete asked, amazed. "We get 'em all the time in California. Must not have 'em back east. Here." He broke off a generous piece. "Try it."

It was snow-white outside, the interior dark fudge. Biting into it, I tasted a flavorful combination of peanuts, almonds, caramel, and nougat covered with that thick layer of hard, white chocolate fudge around the soft center. I'd never bought a candy bar outside of Illinois and felt my horizons expanding almost as much as on my recent acid trip. Or maybe I was just hungry.

Our next stop was at the American Indian Center in Gallup. A serene young white guy, the only person there at the time, let us in with a shout.

"Hey! Good to see you guys. How'd it go out there?" He'd been sweeping the floor but set the broom aside to embrace Jim, then Pete, before extending his firm handshake to me. He was introduced to me as a fellow student of Native Indian culture and the natural environment. He lived at the center in exchange for doing odd jobs and offered the same deal to me.

"If you're interested, Ron, I bet you could probably stay here too, meet people, get to know the Indians, and become part of this great landscape." He laughed, nodding his head. "These people can teach us a lot."

It was a tempting offer. I'd long been convinced that the growing white youth movement needed to join with Amerindians, as we called them, who were becoming more militant with a resurging pride in their traditions. AIM, the American Indian Movement, had started just the year before, aiming to counteract the erosion of their society. Urbanization, dislocation from traditional tribal networks, and the despair of their continual defeat and disenfranchisement caused too many Indians to fall into alcoholism and suicide, to say nothing of spousal abuse and child neglect. In turning that around, AIM raised the political consciousness and was making demands on the government for generations of broken treaties and neglect.

"I'll think about it," I told him.

This was the sort of thing I'd been dreaming of for years. Gallup could be my base for exploration in the great Southwest, but I was torn about my original plan to join one of the communes. The other guys were driving on to Santa Fe in the morning. If I wanted a ride, I'd have to make the tough choice fast. If I was wiser, I'd have accepted the offer—to my later regret, I put it off.

"First I want to check out those communes springing up in Taos."

Young and confident, I'd assumed that there would be plenty of time to do everything I wanted, tie all my opportunities together and slip into the larger mosaic of history. My rationale was that the Indians were already getting their trip together. I needed to help my own people, set ourselves up as their allies. We needed to build a viable alternative culture, one that could undermine the establishment that made us all cogs in a mindless social machine. But the road not traveled isn't always easy to backtrack to.

Santa Fe

THE ADOBE FLAVOR OF SANTA Fe captivated me. It had been another long drive from Gallup, and it became hard to part from my companions, but we were sure to meet again. They dropped me in front of a psychedelic head shop in downtown Santa Fe late in the afternoon of the next day. "Someone in there might give you a place to crash," they encouraged me.

I would've been happy for some floor space where I could flop for the night. No one I asked knew about a crash pad, but the long-haired clerk behind the counter advised me to hang out in the music room in back. A couple, arm-in-arm, was leaving as I passed through a portal hung with heavy curtains and strings of psychedelic beads to enter a lounging room without furniture, a place to show off the merchandise. Black lights, alternating with flashing strobes, played over the black-painted walls hung with psychedelic posters. Hindu Yantras and surreal portraits of rock stars like Jimi Hendrix and Janis Joplin leapt out at me, all on sale in the front. Loud, vibrating music, the soundtracks of records also on sale, blasted from huge speakers.

The only person I found was a bearded guy sitting cross-legged against a wall. I sat down beside him and attempted a conversation. "Hi, man, are you meditating?"

His fierce glare told me I'd interrupted his solitary pleasure, so I apologized and told him I was new in town, just trying to find a place to stay.

"Ask somebody else," he snarled as he got up and stalked out.

The record ended; silence ensued. This eerie place was as good as any to meditate. Taking off my combat boots, I crossed my legs into full lotus posture. As if on cue, sound exploded from the speakers.

"AUUUUUUUUMMMMMMM!" The vibration tingled my bones. A sitar instrumental intruded, then again, "AUUUUUUMMMMMM, HEEEEEAAAAVEN."

Om, heaven? It was the Moody Blues, *In Search of the Lost Chord*. Although released in July 1968, this was the first time I heard it. Hearing it at this juncture of my life seemed auspicious, a blessing upon my quest. I opened myself to let the vibe run through me. Hearing the Moody Blues renewed my spirit and faith in the culture. Although this head shop was primarily a business, I saw no firm line between the sacred and profane. There was no life without eating; the owners had to make a buck or vanish. Mass marketing music with the right message had an accidental result of stimulating fresh ideas in at least some consumers. This shop had become sacred ground with great potential as a rendezvous for wandering shamans and seekers like me.

People came in and squatted nearby, tripping on the psychedelic effect of the music and light show. After being put off by the first guy, I'd decided to ignore people, let them approach me if they wanted. Sure enough, after another song or two, somebody nudged me.

"Hey, man, I heard you're Taos bound and need a place to crash." He led me outside by the back door and pointed up a graveled alley. "There's some dudes hangin' out in a driveway up there. They're going to Taos in the morning, and I bet they'll take ya."

Taos! My destiny was falling into place. The alley was devoid of streetlights, and it was already too dark to see far. The distant sound of coarse laughter led me toward shadow figures lit only by the faint glow of cigarettes. They seemed to be the ones I'd been directed to find. As I got closer, I made out their speech, which was punctuated with harsh, vulgar curses like *shit, goddamn,* and *motherfucker* that carried on the night air far better than softer words. Closer in I smelled pungent reefer along with the tobacco they were smoking.

I felt as if I were passing from an ethereal dimension into a lower realm, from the sanctity of a room purified by the mantra *om* into the harsh world of *Samsara*. With determined steps I trudged on into the outer darkness of deluded beasts called men. From among them I'd seek my next companions on the way.

In a circle of younger guys standing beside a car parked in a driveway, I found a stubble-faced, mustachioed man in his mid to late twenties wearing a fringed, brown leather jacket. His wide-brimmed safari hat was turned rakishly up at one side; his unkempt hair hung down in tangled snarls to his shoulders. He'd been holding forth with a booming voice to the rapt attention of his male companions. As I approached his voice boomed out at me.

"Who the fuck're you, man?" As if he thought I was a narc or something.

"Like, I heard you guys are going to Taos, and I was wondering if you had room to take me along?"

"Who the *goddamn fuck* told you that?" His response left me wondering if I'd found the right bunch or if I should keep going but I brazened it out.

"This guy over at the head shop told me, man."

"What does he *fucking* think I am? A *goddamn* bus?"

Everybody laughed, and I felt some of the tension subside. One of the others extended his arm my way. "You wanna hit, man?" He offered me a joint, and I inhaled deeply and passed it along. Their suspicion became allayed by my toking up, partaking of the herb with them.

"Yeah, he's cool," their leader said. "Let him stay, fuck it!" Thus, I was accepted onto the fringe of their fellowship.

This leader was nothing if not an exhibitionist. He gesticulated wildly as he launched into the recounting of one madcap adventure after another, and the hero was always himself. Cursing was a big part of his performance; almost every other sentence was punctuated by a profanity. It was *goddamn* this and *fucking shit* that as he flailed his arms about in fast, jerking movements. He was a caged lion, on edge, as if impatient to be somewhere, almost anywhere else. He kept repeating that he wanted to "split from this goddamn city" and "tomorrow won't come *goddamn* soon enough, fucking hell!"

Listening to him ramble on, I learned something of the local lore where I was going. He talked of the "*goddamn* Buddhist Lamas" who he claimed lived high up on a mountain on the far side of Taos. They had gongs made from the bomb casings they'd found in the

Los Alamos atomic bomb range. That was *fucking* unbelievable, he said. They'd bang on these gongs with hammers to call themselves to assemble for prayer or meditation. One dark night he'd sneaked up there with a friend and rung them loudly before running into the trees, just to see if the *goddamn* monks would come racing down the mountain to see what was up.

It was a fantastic story, but what was even more amazing, I later learned that his bizarre story was true. The place was the Lama Foundation; he'd gotten the Lama part right. It was an interdisciplinary spiritual commune that I later came to know well.

Later that year I saw the movie *Easy Rider* and recognized the character played by Dennis Hopper as almost identical to this outrageous fellow. They'd done much of their filming around Taos, and the actor Dennis continued to live in the area. To this day I wonder if they'd modeled Dennis Hopper's character on him or if this fellow was Dennis in the flesh.

"You need a place to crash, huh?" Dennis Hopper's doppelgänger finally asked me. "Okay, man, you can stay here tonight. It's not really my place but *fuck* him anyway!"

Fuck who, I wondered? Then he launched into the story of how he'd just been bailed out of jail there in Santa Fe. I never learned the cause of his incarceration, but his story went that, of all things, a Trappist monk had posted his bond. I assumed he was bullshitting us until I met this quiet little ex-monk, who confirmed the main outline of the story.

"I don't give a shit, whatever *his* fucking problem is," Easy Rider boasted. "I'm not paling up with that goddamn pansy of a monk—no fucking way!"

It shocked and offended me how Easy talked so callously about his benefactor. Instead of gratitude, he derided the monk as nothing but a goddamn do-gooder whose solicitous interest in his welfare was cramping his macho lifestyle, even though he was camping in the monk's place and probably eating his food. Maybe the monk should have left this clown to rot in jail.

One of the guys wanted to get a pack of cigarettes, and I walked around the corner to the store with him. "That's the Trappist monk," he told me, pointing to a short, unassuming fellow standing in the checkout line. His head was still partly shaved in a monkish tonsure. He even wore a robe, as if to proclaim that he was still in the religious life, even if he remained out in the world helping people.

"Yes," the somber fellow admitted. He'd lived the Trappist life of silence and prayer, but something was missing. He'd begun debating whether the simple contemplative life was his calling. The fallen world was reeling him back, but its taste was bittersweet, leaving him undecided. Maybe he'd return to the monastery and then again, maybe not.

"Did you ever read *The Seven Story Mountain* by Thomas Merton?" he asked me. That had been his inspiration to become a Trappist.

"Yeah, some of my Catholic friends had been bugging me to read it." In truth I'd thumbed through a copy in their little Catholic library. I found Thomas Merton more interesting and open-minded than most of the other Catholic *dog-mentists*. Merton struck me as a kind of Buddhist Catholic. Like this monk, he'd also given up the sequestered life of contemplation after going toe to toe with his ecclesiastical superiors. As I recalled, Merton had died suddenly on a trip to Asia, where he'd been seeking to build bridges of equality and mutual respect with adherents of other faiths. Expanding his horizons: that was something rare in a Christian.

This monk who'd bailed out the loudmouth Easy seemed so alone, a forsaken man, treading his own austere spiritual path. He still needed the warmth of a fellow human's touch. He'd been looking for love in all the wrong places, as had Christ and Buddha, because those were the actual places in which humans existed. His was a Bodhisattva attitude, treading a path of self-abnegation for the sake of saving all. As for his would-be Easy Rider friend, I couldn't help wondering what kind of karma that renegade hipster was creating for himself.

Back at the driveway, Easy clapped his hand on my shoulder, startling me with his sudden familiarity. "Hey, man, you still wanna go to Taos with us in the morning?"

"Sure, man, if you got room."

"Okay then, fuck, we'll squeeze you in, but we can only take you partway. The people there, they don't want me bringing no goddamn strangers up to bug 'em. See?"

Easy was spontaneous, loud, and obnoxious, but he could be charming and generous too, reminding me of some of the tough Greasers I'd known back home. Their actions were often unpredictable, and I'd gotten used to walking a fine line with my fellow humans. Easy wasn't such a bad a guy—I could handle him.

They referred to their commune in Taos only as *the farm*, and they wouldn't say where it was, as if afraid I'd track them down. I gathered that it was some distance beyond Taos out in the mountains. They spoke of a place called New Buffalo that had been the first hippie commune in the area. Others followed throughout the region, made up of a wide variety of personalities, from the industrious to the selfish and lazy who took more than their share. This created conflict that had caused most communes to become unwelcoming by the time I came on the scene.

These New Mexican hippies were by no means the gentle peace-and-love folk of the tabloids, open to accepting strangers. But I'd been an outsider all my life. Getting into Taos would only be my first step to explore as many places as I could. I'd try to ingratiate myself into whichever one fit.

"Those goddamned Chicanos!" Easy spit out the words, the preamble to another speech.

Chicanos? It was a word I'd heard only a few months ago on the TV news. They were Mexican descendants who'd been born in the United States. Many in the Southwest even claimed descent from the conquistadors. Those conquerors of the Pueblo Indians then lost the country to the Anglo-Americans in the Mexican War. The new regime of *Gringo* Americanos didn't honor their Spanish land grants nor respect their Catholic culture after more English-speaking immigrants flooded in.

In the 1960s Chicanos began battling for their land grants anew. In 1967 they raided a courthouse that had ruled against their claims. This event, although not given a lot of press, fired me with hope for a common front with all oppressed people. I was for tolerance and equality. My sympathies were with the conquered people of all races who could recognize the common good, but the battle lines were blurring. The new wave of Anglos, half-naked hippies who championed versions of brotherhood and cooperation, found themselves acquiring land whose ownership was disputed by the Chicanos, adding insult to injury instead of a solution.

Easy gave us the lowdown on the simmering culture war going on between the hippies and some of the locals. So far, all the violence came from the locals. Shots had been fired, he claimed, a few hippie women had been gang-raped, some hippie cabins dynamited. It looked like the turf war was heating up.

It was ironic. How could hippies have ended up on the oppressor side of history? To the Catholic Chicanos the hippies were an unwelcome intrusion of alien values. As for the Native Americans, the picture became even more confusing. Many were socially and culturally mixed with the Chicanos, but they had their own issues of disenfranchisement dating from the Spanish and Mexican era. American Indians were experiencing a reawakening of their own pride, while in the background some Chicanos prided themselves on being pure Spanish with no Indian blood. I found myself in an extraordinary place where passionate people engaged in larger-than-life issues that I'd have to investigate further when I got there.

Easy bragged that they would be up by the crack of dawn, telling me I'd goddamn well better be ready, or they'd leave me behind. We all plunked down wherever we found a spot to sleep in the house, me on the living room floor. Come late morning, much later than the dawn's early light they'd bragged about the night before, ill-tempered and groggy, my acquaintances slowly roused themselves. I'd been up much earlier, patient and meditating, keeping out of their way until the motley assembly had dug in on a partially burned pot of pinto beans and day-old bread. These stalwarts breakfasted on little else besides stale coffee and water. My share was the remainder, sans bread, which was gone by that time.

It felt good to have something in my belly, but I didn't get enough, so I finished the cold, gritty coffee, drank much more water to wash down the burnt beans, and filled up my canteen for the road.

The sun was high in the sky, close to noon, before they were ready, but at last we all jammed into the overloaded car. Five, including me, crammed in the back and four in front made for a tight squeeze, our painful knees pressed together, giving me a prickling sensation as my circulation closed off, but at least we were Taos bound!

"Goddamn it," groaned Easy more than enough times. "Why the fuck did I agree to take *all* you assholes with me? I could a driven in comfort, you know. Guess I'm too goddamn kind-hearted for my own good. Maybe that goddamn monk knew what he was doing when the fucker bailed me out. Huh? I'm a fucking saint, like him!"

Everybody in the car burst out laughing, which caused us to bump into each other, but we were delirious, beyond pain or numb to it. It was about seventy goddamn miles to Taos, and all we had to do was grit our teeth and get there. Easy drove like a maniac, somehow shifting gears while *goddamning* the bruised knees that got in his way. But everything comes to an end eventually. They dropped me some distance below Taos and took a side road to the northwest.

Trudging north on Highway 68, I wondered if all the local hippies were as arrogant and crude as those I'd met so far. Would I even find my way to a commune? And if I did, would I be accepted? Not if they were all as suspicious of strangers as Easy and his friends claimed. Maybe I, the eternal outsider, wasn't hip or cool enough for any of them.

A car pulled over and honked, breaking into my troubled thoughts. The dark-complexioned fellow appeared to be about forty years old. He had an accent, possibly Mexican, and a trim little black mustache. I told him straight out that I wanted to visit the communes that were blossoming all over Taos. He laughed and said he knew quite a few of them, but because of the rapid influx of wandering youths like me, they were becoming choosy about who they let stay.

"Most of these newcomers don't even stay long enough to make an initial investment of time and food worthwhile. The better organized places will give you a probationary period, then kick you out if you don't measure up to their standards."

"That sounds okay to me. Really, I'm serious about sticking around."

"Good. These communes, you know, come in all shapes and sizes. What exactly are you looking for? A place where you can cop out and just get high without any responsibility, or a place where you could make a difference in the world?"

"I'm a hard worker, man. I want to be part of something grander than a crash pad."

"All right, I've got the perfect place for you, son. I'll take you straight there instead of dropping you off somewhere in downtown Taos. Who knows where you'd end up then?"

Everything was working out due to this helpful guide. Our conversation turned to the hippie war. He began raving about *those goddamned Mexicans around here.* "They want to be called Chicanos, of all the idiotic things! Everyone knows Chicano is a disparaging term, like nigger. These goddamn, lazy *Beaners* want to be just like fucking niggers!"

His sudden rant confused me. Up until then I'd thought *he* was Mexican. Maybe he was, with a gripe against some of his own people. Or maybe this was a trick? I read a lot of spy stories. What if he was a Chicano agent provocateur, baiting me to see where my sentiments lay? Or maybe he was just a sunburnt European and a racist one at that.

Hitchhiking is always a gamble. My toss of the dice had landed me with another volatile personality, like Easy. The country seemed full of them. He had a lot to get off his chest, but whoever he was, he appeared to be helping me. I nodded noncommittally as he gesticulated and pounded the steering wheel while delivering his passionate monologue as if he was a dictator.

"The goddamned Chicanos," he continued, "can't see the tremendous economic benefits of allowing the hippies into this poor, dry country. The hippies could only add to the economy here. They're buying land, generating business, creating wealth! The stupid Chicanos can only hold on to their outdated traditions, which keeps them from moving into the twentieth century. Instead of progressing, they cry over their grievances and miss their golden opportunity in the here and now."

I wasn't used to hearing older, straight guys heaping praise on hippies, much less touting them as good for the economy. What a paradox, to hear of hippies as shock troops in an ethnic conflict. It ran counter to everything the counterculture was supposed to stand for. Being new in the country, I muffled my own opinions and listened. The Taos scene was too complicated for an instant assessment.

He turned left at Rancho de Taos, about four miles short of Taos proper, then turned left again on a gravel road that dipped down, then up over a small, wooden bridge that spanned an irrigation ditch. It was shaded like a mini oasis under cottonwood trees.

"They call these ditches *acequia*, and the local community organization puts strict control over who gets the water and when. In this dry country water is everything. The snow melt coming off the mountains needs to be channeled in for crops."

We arced through a curve and came to a halt in front of a fenced-in, modern-looking, pink adobe house. "This place," he proclaimed, "is the Sound Current Ranch of Rancho de Taos. Come on, I'll introduce you to the man in charge."

Stranger in a Stranger Land

"HOWDY, JOE, ANYBODY HOME?" THE ranter shouted as he led me inside the spacious living room, as if assured of admittance. A group of about six short-haired, collegiate-looking young men and three modest young women sat around the rug-strewn floor at the feet of a much older, bronzed man. His face was lined, his high forehead crowned with long locks of salt-and-pepper hair twisted into a braided tail that stretched far down his back, giving him a Native American appearance.

The ranter introduced me. "Hey, Joe, this kid's looking to join a commune."

"Far out! He's come to the right place." The long-haired man stood up and smiled as he shook my hand, interlocking our thumbs with a firm grip, as was the hippie fashion. "I'm Joe Sage. You'll really *dig* this place, man, it's *far out*." He gave an encouraging wink. "I'm a minister of the Church of Zen Macrobiotics."

Macrobiotics? Zen sounded interesting, but a church? A combination of curiosity and apprehension filled me.

"See," the ranter said. "I told you I'd help get you situated." He immediately backed out and I never saw him again, leaving me to wonder how involved he was with Joe.

"Sit down and make yourself at home," Joe said. "I'm almost done with these kids here."

Joe's deep voice filled the house like an organ in church, except that his speech was an exotic mix of hipster jargon and technical terms that were completely new to me, peppered with vulgar profanities. By then I was getting used to the aggressive, profane speech of the extroverts I met in the Southwest. He extolled his ability to help the whole hippie generation get over its addiction to the unhealthy American diet with the wonders of macrobiotics.

"One thing you will notice eating a macrobiotic diet is you won't need toilet paper. Your shit comes out firm, leaving your ass clean enough to kiss."

That provoked much giggling from the crowd at his feet. His claim seemed far-fetched. Later I found that his modern, tiled bathroom did have a toilet paper roll hung handy, but his claim was true. After a couple days of the brown-rice menu, I had no residue on the toilet paper after wiping my ass. A sign of macrobiotic health.

"Goddamn near everybody from the older generation puts you kids down," Joe said, throwing his arms out as if to hug them all while shaking his head. "But goddamn it, I have great respect for hippies. Your goddamn generation is getting it together with a lot of positive energy. With a goddamn macrobiotic diet, you hippies will transform this whole goddamn country, maybe even the whole fucking world."

His small, collegiate audience may not have considered themselves hippies—maybe they only had an academic interest, intending to write up their findings for a class—but they remained quiet and respectful, if a little uneasy at the force with which Joe delivered his message. I'd have to get used to hearing *goddamn*, an overused word that made me cringe.

"Goddamn it, I'm over fifty goddamn years old and as healthy as any of you young dudes. On a brown-rice diet, I've got more energy than a goddamn twenty-year-old." He winked and a lascivious smile crossed his face. "I'm always goddamn hard and ready too. I can still ball a chick all night long and have plenty left to ball her friend in the morning!"

Ball? He employed the word in an unfamiliar way. Was he referring to the balls swinging between his legs? My tired brain grasped at context; he had to mean *fucking*. Balling, he said, was natural and healthy and not a sin as taught in straight religion. If you didn't ball on a regular basis, your psychic balance would be out of whack, leading to health problems. He rambled on about how essential balling

74

was for a vigorous and healthy life, rejuvenating our bodies as we got older.

"Let me tell you kids, I'm an old man, you say, but with a macrobiotic diet I ball every goddamn night, maybe more than once with more than one chick, and I stay as strong and healthy as any one of you cats."

More tittering erupted from his audience. There was nothing subtle about Joe Sage. Despite the streaks of gray in his hair and his lined face, he looked fit. Did the chicks really go for him, as he implied? He was laying it on thick, flattering these college kids, but from their shocked expressions, especially the girls, it seemed Joe was overdoing it with his sex talk, putting them off rather than reeling them in. It shocked me too, but I was trying to overcome my inhibitions to gain sexual experience, of which I had only secondhand knowledge. Still a virgin, I was horny as fuck. Maybe this place could solve my problem.

There was a dictum current among hippies that went, *Don't trust anyone over thirty*. Although I was at odds with my parents, I never believed in a war between the generations. We were all in the same boat: planet Earth. We had to work together with everyone who recognized this and had an intelligent understanding. If older, wiser, and more experienced men, like Joe Sage, were ready to help us transform the *goddamn* world, it would be for the best. I'd left home because I wanted to promote human evolution, and anyone with an open heart and a clear vision was cool by me. I wanted to believe that Joe was sincere and trustworthy.

A pretty blond woman spoke up. "Could you please tell me more about the spiritual retreats you're hosting here?"

"Sure. A big crowd will be coming here this summer. Too many to fit inside, so we'll set up tents for the overflow on the field. You should sign up now or stay over a few days and get to know this transformative philosophy. You might be persuaded to join our family once you get to know us."

The earnest young people wrapped up their questions, said they were glad to have come and grateful for the reception. They had a few more places to check out, but they'd seriously consider all that they'd heard and maybe be back soon. Joe tried to pin them down as to when that would be, but they wouldn't say. As they left, I took their place on the Navajo rug at Joe's feet, wondering if I really ought to commit myself to this place or split with them.

No sooner were they out the door than Joe's ingratiating smile left his face, and he began lambasting them. "Those goddamn college punks, all they do is look but don't want to get involved. Goddamn pansies! They don't even have the fucking guts to put their ideas into practice."

His sudden anger shocked me. It seemed at odds with his claim to be a spiritual guru, but I'd been reading about great Tantric yogis, like Tilopa and Marpa, who used anger as a skillful means to blast disciples onto the lightning path to Buddhahood, and Zen had similar tales. Could Joe be my karmically destined guru? I'd keep an open mind. Although, like the departing students, I preferred to check out other communes before committing myself, I'd have to spend a few days to get to know each, and I might as well start there.

"So you want to live on a commune?" Joe asked rhetorically. "Do you think you can commit to stick it out here?"

I nodded affirmation.

"Good, because we need people who have what it takes—guts, not some goddamn tourists like those goddamn kids!"

Less than an hour ago I'd been dumped off on the road with the warning that most Taos communes were clannish and didn't welcome strangers. It had seemed difficult to get accepted. Suddenly my luck had reversed. It looked like I was being welcomed as an asset to this macrobiotic commune, whatever that was. I'd see how this played out before I made a final decision.

Joe gave a good-natured laugh. "I'm a full-blooded Blackfoot Indian, you know." He thumped his puffed-out chest and fixed me with a sincere-yet-defiant gaze.

I wondered if he expected me to challenge him. I knew the Blackfoot Indians were from Montana and Canada. He was far off the tribal reservation, but I was also far from my origins. People from everywhere were on the move.

Joe rambled on, telling me that he was a Zen monk, a beatnik, a farmer, a restaurateur, you name it, before he'd become a mentor to the hippie generation. He owned the Good Karma Macrobiotic Restaurant in LA or Frisco, I forget which. Both cities were just words to me at that time. As a follower of Edgar Cayce, the "Sleeping Prophet," I expected that California would soon slide into the ocean. It behooved me to steer clear of the West Coast.

The Good Karma, Joe explained, had been left in the hands of his partners while he'd come to Taos only a month ago to set up his macrobiotic commune. Joe was convinced that his partners were ripping him off and running his restaurant into the ground. But as he kept repeating, he was *fifty-one goddamn years old*. He hadn't sold his soul for a nine-to-five job. No, he'd filled his life with meaningful experience that he was ready to pass on to my fortunate generation.

His spiel of self-promotion was sprinkled with terms I hadn't heard before. Words like *grok* and *Sanpaku* were mixed in with too-frequent exclamations of *far out*, but never *groovy* or *out of sight*, terms which must have become obsolete, as he made a disgusted face when I used them. I'd been wandering in the desert, spending too much time alone, and there I was, being overwhelmed by a brand-new vocabulary. Joe asked if I *grokked* what he'd been telling me.

Grokked? I guessed it meant something like *dig*, the hippie word for like or to understand something. Not wanting to appear an imbecile, I said, *Sure, I grok it*. Sanpaku would be explained later. Joe's flash of anger at the departed visitors transformed into warm passion as he explained that his ranch was an expanded family where they were all married to each other. They were all *one* and had to overcome jealousy and learn to share everything, even each other's bodies. Us guys could ball any one of our chicks. He watched my reaction to that.

The idea excited me but as the stranger wandering into new situations, I'd gotten used to masking my feelings, never certain how they'd be received.

"What's the matter? Don't that goddamn shit sound good to you?"

"Yeah!" I tried to show more elation. "Far out, man, it sounds great."

I grokked the sex part. Although I hadn't seen any girls yet, I didn't want to miss my chance by seeming disinterested. I was well read about sex but still inexperienced, aside from a few make-out sessions and some exhibitionist stripping that my almost-girlfriend had beguiled me and my friends with in junior high. That taste of happiness seemed so long ago, and I was damn sick of my virginity, ready for the real thing. Joe didn't say anything about dudes balling each other. Fine by me because it wasn't my bag. I wasn't gay and was tired of dissuading guys who hit on me.

Joe assigned me a book to read: *You Are All Sanpaku* by George Oshawa. The science of macrobiotics had everything to do with food. Sanpaku described a condition in which the whites of the eye appeared between the pupil and the lower lid. That is, the lids hung low, bagging under the eyes. It connoted a state of physical and spiritual imbalance. The affected person was out of touch with his or her body and the natural forces of the universe. Sanpaku was marked by chronic fatigue, low sexual vitality, poor instinctive reactions, bad humor, inability to sleep soundly, and a lack of precision in thought and action. Scary shit!

Later I looked in the mirror for signs of this condition. I looked okay but only if I held my head directly forward. According to George, foods fell into two categories: yang, or masculine, and yin, or feminine. A healthy ratio was a diet that balanced about 80 percent yang to 20 percent yin. Brown rice was the perfect food; beginners were recommended to live on it entirely for a few days, weeks, or even months in order to clean out the system and correct the internal imbalance caused by a lifetime of wrong eating. Then, the toxins cleaned out, they could add other foods, like adzuki beans or miso soup and vegetables, and other properly balanced items.

We were admonished to avoid sugar like poison. Ideally one got by with little or no commercial condiments or seasonings that contained any sugar or other sweeteners. Over time our taste buds would adjust to the natural flavors of wholesome foods, and then if we tried

it, we'd find sugar distasteful. There were a variety of approved top-
pings made from seeds and beans, like tamari and sesame butter.

Strangely, I was also told to drink teas and not much plain water,
but I much preferred clean, cold water. Acceptable macrobiotic beverages included something called Mu tea. Could that exotic beverage
come from the ancient lost continent of Mu? I'd been doing a lot of
reading about the lost continents of Atlantis and Mu. Mu, also called
Lemuria, had sunk under the Pacific Ocean. Much of my informa-
tion came from Edgar Cayce, the Sleeping Prophet, whose books I'd
been studying. He also had a dietary system, stressing a low ratio of
acidic to alkaline foods. There was a certain amount of correlation
between the two systems, but I also saw some glaring inconsistencies.
Cayce recommended drinking plenty of water.

Joe mentioned opening his *third eye* and his proficiency at astral
projection, leaving his body in a spirit form. He had big plans for
the Sound Current Ranch, conducting seminars to lead students
into higher spiritual dimensions while teaching his alternative to the
dreadful American junk-food diet.

The way Joe monopolized the conversation, I hadn't much of
a chance to get a word in. I'd need time to absorb some of the ideas
and terminology winging past me, but I'd stick around long enough
to see how Joe's Love Tribe worked.

A blue-and-white VW van pulled into the driveway, and a crew-
cut, sandy-haired guy in his early twenties came in. With an almost
military precision, he reported to Joe about how work on the restaurant and clinic was progressing.

"Far out," responded Joe. "Jeff, this is Ron, our new family
member. Introduce him to the others. Just be goddamn sure to stop
over at La Clinica first." Turning to me, he said, "That's our free
clinic." Back to Jeff, "See if they need anything and when the doctors
are ready to open."

We hopped in the VW and drove north into Taos. Without
cursing even once, a welcome change from the past two days, Jeff
explained the family philosophy. Each of *us*—and it gratified me that
he was already including me in the *us*—slept together in a common
room. The girls were compliant, eager for sex to our mutual satis-

faction. The attractive concept inflamed my mind; a dream that I'd nourished forever was finally to be fulfilled. Should I mention that I was a virgin?

At my age my dick got hard even when it was inconvenient to have my pants tented out in obvious arousal. I needed a place to put it but worried about making a fool of myself by doing something wrong and spoiling my chance. Therefore, I decided to see how things went and take my cue. Unless a girl took the initiative. Wow, that would be terrific!

I was anxious to meet these mysterious ladies and couldn't help wondering whether the women in this arrangement were attractive or ugly, but I wouldn't be picky. Raised on airbrushed *Playboy* centerfolds, I had recently broadened my appreciative lust for the great variety of bodies that womankind offers.

Jeff continued, "Did you ever read Stranger in a Strange Land?"

"No. Isn't it that science fiction novel by Heinlein?"

"Yes, that's our Bible. That's where the word *grok* came from. Here." He reached into the back seat and rummaged around while steering with his left hand until he found it. "Take my copy and read it. You'll grok it, man."

Thus, I had two books to absorb when I had time. Although I preferred nonfiction, I had friends deep into sci-fi, and they'd filled me in on the storyline. Robert A. Heinlein's 1961 book is about a Martian-raised human who comes to Earth, bringing with him Martian words and a unique perspective on the strange ways of Earthlings.

Maybe the Bible, the Koran, and the Bhagavad Gita were all works of fiction, but I felt they were attempts at honesty, even if based on exaggerated perception and misremembered myths as facts. After skipping around reading what were supposed to be the good parts in the next few days, I dropped it. My real life had become much more interesting than wading through the book.

Taos was a combination of older adobe architecture that gave the place some class, and Kit Carson might recognize parts if he came back, but ugly glass-and-metal commercial buildings marred the illusion. The Conoco gas station was one such landmark. Jeff turned onto a dusty, unpaved gravel road, then pulled into a wide, sandy parking lot and stopped before a one-story line of fake adobe storefronts.

La Clinica was painted in bold letters above the glass door and picture window, a plank sidewalk lay in front, and to the left another establishment's bold sign proclaimed: General Store.

"Here," Jeff said, "grab some of these bags," and he led me inside.

One of the doctors who would be donating his time was stocking medical supplies. Jeff asked him if there was anything he needed done. The doctor looked around a moment. "We could use a handrail over here and also there," he said, pointing along the wall. "Because we'll be serving elderly Chicano and Indian people here, not just your young hippie dropouts overdosing on drugs!"

We all laughed, then Jeff told him: "We're not all druggies, you know." Which caused another bout of laughter, although I'm not sure why it seemed so funny.

We rummaged around the remaining odds and ends that constituted the building supplies we'd brought in and came up with some wooden doweling and brackets. I was only too happy to help on the project. Jeff let me install the grab bars while he did something else. Then, after sweeping up, everything looked ready. Several old Indian people were already sitting on folding chairs in the front, hoping for medicinal relief, which the doctor, bound by his Hippocratic oath, dispensed free of charge, even though they weren't ready to officially open.

It warmed my heart to see that we were doing something good for the local people. Maybe the anti-hippie sentiment could be overcome with deeper understanding, and we could all create a common bond.

THE SEVEN PATHS

"OKAY," JEFF SAID. "IT'S TIME for us to go to our restaurant." He gave me a wink. "You'll meet the others there."

We drove to the northern edge of town on the main drag and kept left at a Y intersection. To go right would take us up to the Pueblo. That was the Indian village around which modern Taos had grown. Just two buildings past that intersection, we pulled into a gravel parking lot on the right before a whitewashed structure. Two large, plate-glass windows flanked a beat-up wooden, double door. The windows were covered with bits of tape and stenciled lines in varying stages of being painted with an elaborate mosaic of interconnected astrological symbols.

The roof of the veranda above the entrance was held up by three vertical beams. To complete the Western flavor, two upright wagon wheels sat to either side of the door. Another post held up a large, old, plastic sign, level with the roof. The original words had been painted over to read:

SEVEN PATHS
MACROBIOTIC
FOOD

A small OPEN sign hung below that. Painted to the left of the door was *Tourists Welcome as You Are,* dating from when this had been a Mexican restaurant. It was to be an entirely different establishment now, yet the motto still applied. The bottom line of a business, even one run by hippies, was to make money despite our desire to change the world.

As we drove up, a burly guy and a pretty girl were busy painting the mosaic. They put down their brushes and rushed over to greet us. Then the Spanish-style doors swung open, and another pretty brunette came out, holding a baby. As he put the van in park, Jeff told me these girls, both knockouts by any standard, were our wives.

"No way, man!"

"Yes, way, man! Come on, I'll introduce you."

"Look who I brought," yelled Jeff, stepping out of the van. "This is Ron, Joe says he's one of us now."

The burly guy came up and shook my hand. "I'm Joe," he said. "To avoid confusion with Joe Sage, everyone calls me Little Joe, even though I look more like Hoss than Little Joe Cartwright on *Bonanza*." He elicited our laughter at that reference to the popular TV Western.

There was, however, nothing little about him. Both Joes were about the same height, and if anything, Little Joe was broader and more muscular than the older Joe Sage. Little Joe was about twenty-two years of age, which seemed to be the median age around there. He had a motorcycle and dressed like a hip biker, often with a red bandanna over his long, rusty-brown hair. He wore a pair of leather chaps on occasion and favored denim shirts and pants.

The yellow-blond, California girl with shoulder-length hair took the infant from the dark-haired woman. "Hi, Ron, I'm Tike." She giggled. "It's pronounced like *bike*. This is my son." Tike proudly held up her bundle of joy for me to admire while I pretended not to be paying more attention to her prominent, half-exposed bosom.

"His name is Zon, pronounced as in son, but with a Z, you see. It's a Vietnamese name, which actually means *son*. Isn't that crazy!"

Zon seemed to be about a month old. She handed him over to me, and I was happy to hold the gurgling infant, who began making sucking sounds.

"He's hungry," Tike said as she finished opening the front of her blouse, then pulled out her tits and took him back to nurse. Her unabashed exposure thrilled me. She was comfortable with her body and didn't mind us watching. In fact, she shifted position for me to watch her breasts in action, which gave me a thrill that took me back to archaic memories. Memories of our eternal *Urmutter*, for we have all suckled at that mythic breast for magic moments, shameless, as being needless of shame. In our puritanical society we'd learned to cringe at what is needful and natural. I saw Tike's attitude as heroic and inspiring, certain that we needed more, not less, acceptance of nudity in our daily life to make our culture humane and loving.

Zon was cute and seemed contented, a wise and well-behaved child, which Tike attributed to his diet of breast milk and her complementary diet of pure, macrobiotic food.

Jeff later told me that Little Joe had been, and still sort of was, Tike's old man, although now we were all one big family and husbands and wives to each other. I'm not sure if Little Joe was baby Zon's natural father or if he'd been born before or after their arrival in Taos. Little Joe had ridden out here from California on his motorcycle with Tike hugging him tight all the way. I don't see how they could have managed it on the bike with the baby.

The other woman was Joanne, who'd been babysitting Zon while Tike painted. She appeared more reserved, cooler than Tike's extroverted personality with a lot on her mind. She had an exquisite Elizabeth Taylor face and a voluptuous figure, set off by her sleek, black mane that fell straight and loose far down her back. Joanne had run away from a rich Chinese husband, bringing their toddler son to this non-monogamous family. She occupied herself with domestic chores, relishing her womanly roles in babysitting, baking, and cuddling her boy, who was then napping inside the restaurant.

Tike's green Army jacket was embroidered with mystic symbols. She noticed my interest and pulled me aside as Jeff discussed business matters with Little Joe. One of the symbols was new to me, an orange circle sliced like a pie into eight equal lines. As she rocked Zon into sleep, she explained it to me.

"That's the Navajo pictograph of the hogan. It also represents life on and *within* Mother Earth." She stressed that last part, saying that it was no accident that hogans were made of earth; they represented the proper relationship with our nourishing Earth Mother.

She also had the ever-present hippie peace sign, which conservative right-wingers called the broken cross of the anti-Christ. She had an Egyptian ankh, a cross with an oval on top, symbolizing eternal life and the spiritual survival of death. Then there was the Taoist yin-yang symbol, which looks like the figure "69," a symbol of unity and balance, and very relevant in macrobiotics with its categorization of food into that duality.

She loved and meditated upon Lao Tzu's *Tao Te King*, a Taoist book. Tike was a woman I could talk with about profound mystical topics.

"Ron, do you know about the *I Ching*, the ancient Chinese Book of Changes?"

"Yeah, I looked it over a year ago. Carl Jung wrote a foreword to it that I found interesting. He thought there was something to it, so there must be."

"It helps me make important decisions. I learned how to throw the yarrow sticks to read the hexagrams to divine my future. I promise I'll do it for you one of these days, soon, when we're not so busy. Maybe after we get the restaurant open."

Beach boy-blond Jeff, with his clean-shaven, short-haired, collegiate look, was the least hippie-looking of the bunch. His wardrobe consisted of regulation male clothing, not a tie-dye nor even a paisley among them. He always seemed to have a mellow smile and a good word to say to everyone. I felt I could confide in Jeff. He was a guy looking for answers in his own quiet way, as dissatisfied with society's status quo as the rest of us.

Up to now we had been standing in the parking lot. At last we entered the restaurant, and Little Joe showed me around. "The place was a Mexican restaurant that did a lot of deep frying. We've been working hard, soaking and scraping decades worth of grease off the stove, walls, and cookware before we can even consider what we cook here pure and wholesome. Then we can finally open."

"That's right," Jeff said. "After all, you are what you eat!"

Tike and Joanne showed me how to make meatless soy burgers, made from equal parts ground carrots and soy flour mixed with a fertilized egg or two to hold it together. Eggs found in the grocery store were sterile, unacceptable to macrobiotics. Tike explained it to me in detail.

"To be macrobiotic eggs have to be fertilized by a rooster's sperm. That makes them capable of producing a chick, thereby balancing the chicken's yin with the rooster's yang. Get it? Otherwise an egg is sterile, just a chicken's menstrual period, and you don't want to eat that. Do you?"

One staple was Japanese adzuki beans. We cooked and ate so many of them. I never figured out why, when we were surrounded with wonderful Southwestern varieties. Nothing against the Japanese but I thought we should use more local foods.

Jeff went to pick up Joe Sage. I'd been famished since the skimpy morning breakfast, so I polished off a plate of rice and beans that Tike offered. Still hungry, she urged me to try some delicious-looking sesame balls. It was the first time I tasted that. Despite being sugarless, they weren't bad. I'd get used to them.

"Go ahead, Ron, eat your fill, we can make more."

Thirsty, I went to the sink, but Tike stopped me. "We don't drink water here, it's too yin. Try a little Mu tea instead, it's made from healing herbs." She pointed to a pitcher of cold, leftover tea. My first time for that too.

The taste was heavy and didn't refresh me or cure my thirst like water, which I still craved. Joe Sage had boasted, "You may see me drink an occasional glass of water, but I get most of my liquid from food and a little Mu tea." Oshawa's book claimed our piss should be brown, not light yellow or clear like mine was. In other words, it should contain more waste. That seemed counterintuitive, contradicting much I'd read from other sources, especially Edgar Cayce. He said we need to flush out our kidneys and digestive system. It made sense to me to drink more, not less, water, but I'd try enduring this new regimen and see how I lasted.

The tea was gone, and I was still thirsty, so just as Jeff and Joe Sage popped in, I left my unfinished ball on the table to find something more to drink. In a sour mood, Sage began berating Little Joe for taking so *goddamn* long painting the *goddamn* windows instead of cleaning the *goddamn* grease in the restaurant. Like an unexpected thunderstorm, Sage's rage exploded loud, ruining everyone's high spirits.

"Why can't I rely on any of you to think for yourselves? Goddamn it, we needed to finish fixing this goddamn place and open soon! We need a positive cash flow because I can't support us forever!"

I was taken aback but only half listened because I was still hunting for a drink. Grabbing and gulping down someone's half-empty cup of cold tea, I began working my way back to my spot at the table. Before I got there, Joe stood where I'd been. He thumped the table and shrieked at all of us.

"See what I mean!" He pounced on my half-eaten sesame ball and held it up like a trophy. "Who the fuck left this! You guys are throwing my goddamn food away!"

It had been so peaceful moments before, and it took a while for me to register what was happening. Before anyone could respond, Joe slammed the sesame ball into the garbage barrel with a thud. Such an overreaction from our Zen monk! Only then did I reach my spot and realize that it was *my* food he meant. I was still hungry and would have to take another one. That angered me, an emotion I stifled. I hated wasting food, especially when I was hungry, and he had wasted it while blaming us. Being new, I didn't know how to respond. Looking around, I saw everyone else as dumbfounded as I was.

"You're right, Joe," Jeff finally said with his breezy diplomatic assurance. "We have to be more careful not to waste food. Everything's going to be okay, man."

That smoothed things over. Sage calmed down but uttered no apology. We filed out to the van and headed back to the ranch. I toyed with the idea of owning up to the sesame ball and telling Joe he'd grabbed it too soon, but the moment had passed, and I was still feeling my way into this group, eager to enter the marriage part of it and didn't want to blow it.

It was obvious that Sage had an anger problem as bad as my old man. I'd already had more than enough screaming psychodrama in my life. If it wasn't for the others I'd just been introduced to, especially the women, I'd take off immediately, but these wonderful ladies were too beguiling to pass up. I'd stick around for my chance at a relationship.

There had to be more to Joe than I saw, otherwise I couldn't see how they could put up with him. Maybe his outburst was only an aberration caused by stress, but it didn't say much for his vaunted macrobiotic philosophy.

FAMILY LIFE

THE SOUND CURRENT RANCH WAS no hippie crash pad or rustic hogan. A wooden fence enclosed a tiled courtyard at the front entry. An interesting collection of antique bottles was stacked along the inside of the fence. Joe seemed proud of them, saying the previous owner had dug them up at dumps, old homesteads, and ghost towns. Joe pointed out how some bottles had bleached out or changed colors to shades of blue or purple. This was an indication of their antiquity. A ranch presumed cattle but there was no livestock, only plowed fields behind the house.

While most hippie communes and Native people needed to chop wood and pump water outside, this house was immaculate with all the modern conveniences: plumbing, toilets, and showers. It was almost too comfortable. The windows had stained glass and prisms hung around the house, bringing in colorful sunshine to dance along the walls. At almost seven thousand feet above sea level, the temperature of Taos fluctuated between hot and a dry cold. The house had an electric heating system, the first of its kind I'd seen. Little indentations in the walls of each room held coils that burned red-hot. We could sleep naked in comfort.

The most prominent piece of furniture was Joe's electric piano. Electric guitars and organs I knew of, but I'd never heard of an electric piano. In an expansive mood, Joe showed off his artistry that first day with his unique sound. He got into it like he was pounding out sacred hymns, his bronzed face contorted with passion, transporting him into far-out dimensions that gave him an angelic glow, as if he were about to levitate.

Enraptured, I recalled my childhood vision of levitation up to a dimly seen face and wondered if this Joe Sage could be the guru who

88

could unlock my spiritual potential. The meditative techniques I'd been studying insisted on remaining calm in all circumstances, to not let wild emotion carry one into extremes of hatred and desire. Those raw emotions were illusions that blocked deeper insight into our cosmic reality, but Joe seemed to be a conduit for extreme passion.

Joe's enchanted music, combined with the colors splashed around the room by the fading sunlight, triggering visions of Edgar Cayce's prophesies, which, in my imagination, combined with what I'd read from American Indian traditions. The lost continent of Mu seemed to be reemerging. We, the reincarnation of her drowned children, were being drawn to the Four Corners region by our karma. Subconscious forces were pulling us together for another try at building a better society, one based not on greed but on spiritual insight. I felt I was in the right place and right time to help fulfil this destiny.

When Joe finished, he fixed his probing gaze on me. "How'd you grok it?"

"It was pretty cool, man," I said, unsure how else to convey my appreciation.

That lukewarm answer didn't please him; I must have appeared too dispassionate. He slammed shut the keyboard and stood up in a huff. "Some goddamn kids can't appreciate this sound."

It would be hard for me to grok this complicated man who had invited me into his family. Would I belong or was I to be ostracized? As an outsider entering a new society, I had to be observant and careful.

"Everyone sleeps together," Jeff said as he led me into the common bedroom. Seven mattresses lay side by side, all the way to the far wall. There was another bedroom too, for the children and extra people. I gathered you could find privacy there if you needed it.

"Which one should I sleep on?" I asked Jeff.

"Wherever you want, there's no assigned spot."

The longed-for bedtime had arrived with its promise of sex. Joanne put all my clothes in the washer while I took a much-enjoyed hot shower. With a towel around my waist, I entered the bedroom. No one else was there yet. Unsure how to comport myself, I picked the mattress at the far end next to the wall, the better to take my cue from what the others did rather than to make a fool of myself. One by one the others trooped in. Joanne took a place at the far wall, then Sage on the mattress beside her, then Tike beside Little Joe, and then Jeff, who slept closest to me.

It was too quiet. I waited with bated breath for something to happen. Without being too obvious about it, I raised up on one arm and looked over the prone forms of my new family for any sign of activity. Nothing. Each of them had gone right to sleep, a disappointing anticlimax, but I supposed they were as tired as I. Exhausted from my long journey, I surrendered to catch some rest myself.

In the predawn hour throaty moans and a heavy thumping that shook the floor awakened me. Raising my head, I saw a naked Joe Sage on top of Tike, slamming into her with all the abandoned gusto of a wild man. His neck craned up, his lips curled like a Billy goat in rut while he grunted like a pig, and his long hair flung free, flopping over his shoulders with each of his rapid thrusts. Tike's legs encircled him, pulling his torso in with each thrust; her gasping cries were punctuated by a soft moaning. Theirs was a primal, impassioned melody created anew from our ancestral storehouse. Everyone else lay still, flat on their backs as if asleep, although I doubted anyone could slumber through the banging drama taking place in our midst. Rising higher, I saw the eyelids of the other two men pressed too tight for authentic sleep. They had to be as discreet as I, enjoying the show.

A peculiar odor hung in the air: the aroma of warm milk that, in their hard coupling, had been pounded from Tike's ample breasts to soak them both in nectar. Even without that exertion, Tike's breasts often leaked a little, meaning that they were full, ready for Zon to suck his nourishment from them.

Admirable savages, these adulterous lovers, I thought. I could only applaud their magnificent performance. The sight took me back to imagined atavistic gatherings, the bangs of gangs in ancient caves, when the young watched their elders romp with neither guile nor guilt. Adults displayed themselves with pride and fulfilled their natural lust.

With a grunt, Sage finished pumping himself into Tike and rolled off to lie on the other side, next to Joanne. After they caught their breath, I heard a few muffled words; it sounded like Joanne and Joe's voices on one side and Little Joe and Tike on the other. Then total silence ruled.

Was this my cue to crawl over and grab some of the action? I should have been bold, but caution and inexperience froze me. Jeff and Little Joe lay between me and Tike. I would have to crawl over them to reach her. Joanne, the only other woman, was again in Joe's arms. I wondered if Little Joe had already balled Tike and if old man Joe had come over to Tike after first balling Joanne. If so, I'd missed it. Had Jeff been innocently sleeping all this time, or did he already have his share? I felt left out but I only had my desperate, prurient imagination to enlighten me on the multiple possibilities of coupling here.

Was there really no jealousy? Through slatted eyes I observed Tike's old man, Little Joe, for signs of wakefulness and emotion. Would he mind if I climbed over him to slide into the warm embrace of either Tike or Joanne? I still didn't understand how I could fit into this group marriage without upsetting someone.

Dawn broke, time to rouse ourselves for a day of labor. The rancid smell of sour milk bore witness to what I'd seen. Tike's stale lactation remained in the air with other pungent odors that had begun to smell of home until Joanne laundered Tike's sheets after breakfast.

Later that day I overheard Joe bragging to Jeff about being drenched with her milk every time he balled Tike. That proved the benefits of a macrobiotic diet for a woman's lactation. Then Joe claimed he feasted on Tike's milk, drinking it right from her jugs either during or after balling. It seemed gross to me then, even though I was a breast man.

New tastes and ideas take a while to adjust to. According to macrobiotics, cow's milk was unfit for humans. A woman's milk was ideal, goat milk a close second. Mother's milk was recommended as a tonic for aging men. No wonder Joe bragged about his sexual stamina. Tike's cups overflowed with more than enough nectar for her son. The surplus bounty that spilled during her amorous encounters became a luxurious salve on their skin, like I'd read Cleopatra enjoyed.

Breakfast always meant plain oatmeal, unless flavored by a few black raisins; the ubiquitous Mu tea, our anytime beverage, washed it down. Mu tea's blend of herbs had a pungent flavor, but I missed plain freshwater, the only thing that cured my thirst. Breakfast was time for the family to plan the affairs of our day.

"Ron," Joe addressed me, "do you know anything about irrigation?"

"Not much, just that water flows along ditches into the field, but I'm willing to learn."

"Okay, you'll work here with me. Joanne will do house duty; the others will go work on the restaurant."

In the shed Joe grabbed a hoe and handed me one before he took off running in his dog-eared sandals across the plowed ground. Green shoots that I tried to avoid sprouted from the tops of ridges between long ditches. Suddenly I felt dazed, lightheaded, and became winded too easily. Maybe I wasn't used to the higher altitude. Exhausted, I struggled to keep up.

"Watch the goddamn plants, will you!" Joe bellowed over his shoulder. "You're breaking down the mounds, messing up all our hard work!"

Despite almost falling over with each step, I was being extra careful watching where I landed. I saw the green shoots and was certain that I hadn't stepped on any, but I was never able to please Joe. The day had become a nightmare; everything I did was wrong.

"I said watch your goddamn feet!" he raged over and over. "You can't see the goddamn things, but I can! And hurry up, goddamn it, time is wasting!"

His lambasting only made things worse. Even when I put my feet *exactly* where Joe's had been, he still yelled that I was stepping on his precious plants, like he had eyes in the back of his head. Overwhelmed and winded, my reactions became more confused and sluggish the more he fumed at me. I was doing my absolute best but not in top form. Maybe Joe was playing a mind game on me, an initiation or a freaking test to see what I was made of. Finally, we reached the sluice gate.

"That goddamn majordomo still isn't here," Joe yelled. "He's always so goddamn late. These goddamn fucking Chicanos can't be trusted to be on time!" Joe worried that they'd open the gate and overflow his field if he wasn't around to monitor. That could uproot his crop.

The local majordomo of the irrigation committee maintained the canal or *acequia*, doling out the water flow according to a careful schedule. Each farmer had to be ready to receive only as much water as he was allotted and only when his turn came. At least I had a moment to catch my breath and try to understand what was going on. If only Joe would stop cursing and settle down, I thought, everything would work out.

"Well, goddamn it, they're not here yet, so let's keep working! Deepen all the fucking furrows, like this." Joe proceeded hoeing along his ditches, using the pointed edge of the hoe turned diagonally so that it dug a sharp V. Following his example, I tried, but in my dizzy state I never managed to reach his exacting expectations. My ruts were either too deep or too shallow and never level enough, and I was unable to move fast enough to suit him.

"Come on, goddamn it! Get moving!" Joe kept egging me on, like my abusive dad. I was doing my absolute *goddamn* best. Why hadn't these furrows been readied before today? It seemed that I'd arrived in the nick of time to give him a pair of hands to get this *goddamn* job done on time. Who else would help him? It didn't look like either Little Joe or Jeff was anxious to be out there working beside him. Maybe they'd all had their fair share of abuse.

Joe was shorthanded for all the projects he was trying to run: the restaurant, this tilled land, fixing the clinic, and whatever else that I didn't even know about. Before I'd come it had only been those two men helping Sage with man's work. He ought to at least pretend to be grateful. The women helped in the house and restaurant, cooking, cleaning, and childcare duties. Tike had regular breast feedings to give, and she and Little Joe were artists, determined to make the Seven Paths a real bang-up joint with murals inside and out.

An hour passed as the sun climbed higher, dissipating the morning chill and bringing sweat to our brows. I wasn't sure if our efforts were making things better or worse. It was a hot, sweaty, thankless job that made me thirsty, but the worst of it was Joe's angry profanity. Suddenly he shouted.

"Okay, stop that now and follow me, quick!" We raced back to the sluice gate. A heavyset Chicano man in a serape spoke a few words to him and then moved along the channel to his next client, or *parciante*. Although I was right behind him, Joe yelled out: "Goddamn it! Will you get over here and help me? We're going to open it up, now put your back into it!"

We began turning the stubborn wheel, the sluice gate opened, and water began gushing into Joe's field, rapidly filling our network of ditches. Some overflowed.

"Well, don't just fucking stand there!" Joe screamed at me. "Clear all those goddamned blockages before you drown my plants!"

We ran around hoeing out the soil that had fallen in or not been dug deep or level enough. The part closest to the intake was already inundated before others received any water. It was backbreaking work keeping up with the myriad streams that branched out from the main channels.

We'd finally done all we could; the water filled the garden. After running back to close the sluice gate, we trooped back into Joe's immaculate house. I'd endured his verbal abuse in silence, hoping that there was a point at which Joe's anger subsided, and I'd see a sunnier disposition from this man who had taken me in with such glib promises. He exhibited none of the calm demeanor I expected a spiritual teacher to possess, unless he followed the lightning path of Tantra. Laboring under him left me feeling depressed and incompetent, giving me second thoughts about staying. Maybe I ought to go back to Gallup and the Indian Center.

Joanne had a macrobiotic feast awaiting us. Flashing her faint smile my way was enough to convince me to put up with Joe for at least one more day. Although she served us in a businesslike manner, her body contrived to brush up against mine. Her warmth and her clean, natural scent intoxicated me, making me feel welcome at last. I'd give this untasted group marriage a chance.

That night I showered, took the same spot, and fell into exhausted sleep, never knowing if anyone had sex around me. The next morning, over our macrobiotic oatmeal, Joe's anger vented against us men in a jarring tongue-lashing as he paced before where we sat together on the couch. What riled him was that *no one, I mean none of you goddamn men, has taken it upon himself to mow the goddamn lawn without being told!*

"What's wrong with you goddamn men anyway? Do I have to tell you everything that needs doing?"

He stopped and eyeballed Little Joe, then Jeff, and finally me with an accusing stare. I'd been there two nights, working beside him the whole previous day, and yet he'd included *me* among the other men as incompetent. I didn't know whether to be ashamed or grateful that I belonged with the other men.

"Don't you all have a goddamn mind of your own? Can't you see that something needs doing and just do it? We have to make a good impression on other people who come by here."

"Goddamn it, Joe!" Little Joe shouted back. "We've all been working our asses off at the restaurant every day. I think the kitchen is ready now, and the windows are almost finished. Let's open the fucking thing already!"

"Those goddamn pots are still not clean enough for me to call this a pure macrobiotic restaurant!"

"Oh, yeah?" Little Joe responded. "Tike and I have enough to do at the restaurant, the goddamn lawn is not a priority. See you later!" He stomped off with Tike and Jeff to Taos while Joe took his car to a meeting, leaving me alone in the house. Without specific orders to do so, I knew I had to mow that goddamn lawn.

The lawn was only a small patch of lush, green grass sloping along one side of the house, about thirty by twenty feet. It struck me as a wasteful use of land in the Southwest, where crops needed irrigation and water was at a premium. I was philosophically opposed to the *lawning of America* as a misuse of nature, but shit, if it would create a little peace around here, I decided I'd cut it myself. It seemed we all had to make compromises with our ethics to get our micro-society to work. At least to mollify Joe. I found an old push mower in the shed and feeling a lot more with it than the day before, I set to work mowing the whole lawn before Joe got back. He never said a word about it nor gave any indication that he'd even noticed. That was fine with me. He had to have noticed, and I hoped that he appreciated it in his own cantankerous way, so we'd have some harmony.

The mailman came. One big, legal-size packet was addressed to "The Mad Monk, Sound Current Ranch, Rancho de Taos." Joe often referred to his past as a Zen monk, although I'm not sure how formally he'd been trained or if it was an exaggeration or affectation. The image of the *mad monk* Rasputin and Aleister Crowley popped into my mind. From what I'd already seen, it wasn't far off the mark. When Joe got back and saw the package, he ripped it open, read a few pages, and blew up.

Those *goddamn business partners* of his had sent it. They were trying to take over his Good Karma restaurant. Addressing him as the *Mad Monk* was intolerable sarcasm. He threw the documents on the ground and stomped them while sputtering curses against those vile hippies who couldn't come up with a successful enterprise like his on their own.

Sage remained in a terrible temper afterward, ready to explode at any of us, his loyal retainers, over any real or imagined fault. Little Joe yelled right back at him to shut the fuck up.

For a minute I thought they'd come to blows. Instead Little Joe backed off, pulling Tike along with him into the bedroom. Sage went to his piano to let music calm him. The storm dissipated without resolution.

THE POWER OF YIN

"SHUT UP AND GET OUT of my way, goddamn it." Joe blew up at Joanne's son. "You're a stupid little punk kid, a stupid goddamn little Chinese brat!"

Those angry words, directed at Joanne's son, shocked me. That wasn't the way to relate to any kid. It was bad enough that he vented his rage on us grown men, but the boy was a mere toddler who craved attention. Joe's harsh rebukes sent him bawling to the spare bedroom, where he and baby Zon slept. He'd cry for his mommy when Joe babysat while she was working at the restaurant. You had to expect a kid to do that, but Joe made it worse by shouting and belittling him.

Joe Sage was a complicated guy with a lot of issues. I couldn't help wondering if he picked on the boy for being half-Chinese. Even though Joe told me he was a Blackfoot Indian, I'd learned racism wasn't limited to white Americans; it could cut both ways, even against one's own people. By contrast he doted on baby Zon, extolling his good health as an example of what the macrobiotic diet could do for nursing moms.

Joanne spoke up at our breakfast meeting. "Why are you always yelling at my kid, Joe? You're upsetting him, he needs love and affection."

"The kid's a sniveling, spoiled brat. You've made him into a goddamn momma's boy. He needs more discipline to grow up and be a man, not a whiney little pansy."

Joanne shot back, "If you don't show more kindness to my boy, I'll split."

Joe looked stung and backed into the sofa, where he sat down. With a subdued voice he continued, "That isn't my intention at all.

You know I love your boy. I'll try harder to be more understanding, more of a father to him."

Joanne had won using her power of yin, which may have encouraged Tike to chime in.

"Joe, don't you recognize the constructive value of play and taking time for other things besides work? That's all we do around here!"

"Well, this is a busy time. We need to open the goddamn restaurant soon, you know."

"When will you begin teaching us astral projection? You promised me, Joe!"

"And what about the peyote ceremony?" Joanne asked. "When will that be?"

My ears pricked up. Since I'd been there, I hadn't heard any reference to marijuana or hallucinogens, which were used by almost all the hippies in the region.

Peyote held a special fascination for me, as its use had been incorporated into traditional Native spirituality following the Ghost Dance of the 1890s, when the half-white Comanche chief Quanah Parker became an advocate. The war on drugs made peyote an illegal substance by federal law; however, by organizing as a church, members had gotten around that, claiming it as a sacrament. It was a legal gray area that only protected card-carrying Native American Church members, but I'd heard local authorities in New Mexico ignored it.

Joe began explaining how we had to be patient. He was involved with the Native American Church at Taos Pueblo, and the conductor—or Roadman, as the pastor or priest of the Church was called—would extend a special invitation to properly introduce us to a ceremony with the members of that spiritual path. It was a path not to be entered lightly.

I got the impression that Joe considered peyote a yang substance, otherwise it wouldn't be on our radar. Experiencing the night-long ceremony until the break of dawn under the influence of that cactus sounded like something I needed to do. It gave me another reason to stick around.

Caught between Joanne and Tike, Joe gave in and declared a holiday. We'd take off the rest of the afternoon to explore astral projection, leaving our physical bodies. That gave me some hope that I'd finally met my guru in Joe. After an extended Hatha Yoga session in the living room, Joe had us lie comfortably on our backs, letting our bodies go limp one limb at a time.

"Now tense your right foot, put your mind into each toe individually, then relax it, feel your toes relaxing, relaxing. Let your mind go out of them. Your right big toe. Tense it and feel it relax. The next toe… Now your right calf…right thigh…left calf…" And so on throughout the entire body in excruciating detail until everything was supposedly limp and lifeless.

It was a standard guided meditation. The trouble was by naming each part of the body, I'd became more, rather than less, enmeshed in the body parts and felt myself unable to *lift off* into the wild blue yonder when that suggestion finally came.

"Now feel yourself rising, float up and out of your body, feel the exhilaration. Turn around and look down, you can see your form there below you. Now rise through the roof, see the fields and road, travel along the road…"

Joe took us on a vicarious tour of the house and neighborhood, along the highway into town, before bringing us back to reenter our respective bodies and slowly, slowly reanimate them, body part by part.

"Wow, far out," Tike exclaimed, enthusiastic about her out-of-body experience. "It was so *real* to me."

Jeff, Little Joe, and I stayed mum. I hadn't projected my astral body. Maybe the fault was with my lack of spiritual preparation. More likely Tike only imagined it.

That evening we sat around the living room floor discussing a wide range of things, from yoga to the scriptures of all religions and how they reiterated the same message. I raised the issue of celibacy. Why was sex such a stumbling block in most religions? Not with us, of course, but the major religions had some form of celibate monks or priests and nuns, and even without them there were so many prohibitions placed on sex, even among the non-deist Buddhists. This led us to the Garden of Eden and then to Revelations in the Christian Bible. Joe referred to the serpent guarding the Tree of Knowledge as a veiled reference to the psycho-sexual power of sex. When I pressed for more detail, he put me off, saying he'd go deeper into it later.

As I went to bed, still a virgin, I was pulled both ways: seeking the supernatural while just as eager to enter the carnal realm of sex. In most traditions they're opposites. I had to find a way to merge them because I needed both.

Photo Credit by John Nichols in May 1969

UNREQUITED SEDUCTION

AT THE RESTAURANT JOE STOMPED around, yelling at Little Joe. "Look at this." He held up the huge kettle, bigger than the kitchen sink. "There's still cooked-in grease on this goddamn thing. You've done a goddamn inadequate job, spending far too much time fussing over those goddamn murals!"

Joe flung a long-handled scrub brush over to me, which I caught. "Ron, it's up to you now. Think you can goddamn handle it?" His voice had an edge of sarcasm, implying that *we*, including me, were all incompetent, irresponsible *goddamn artsy-crafty hippies.* "I'm sending Jeff and Little Joe on another job. I've got a meeting with the town council to go to, but when I get back," his eyes bore into me, "I want to see all the goddamn cookware scrubbed shiny clean. Understand?"

I nodded and jumped to it, putting all my effort into finishing this job once and for all, but I would have done it without Joe's s abusive words. They stung me, slamming me back into my childhood with a workaholic father who, like Sage, was impossible to satisfy. Tike and I had to finish cleaning up the place to his expectations so we could open, but as a woman and a mother and, most importantly, Joe's ready consort, she never got the browbeating that seemed to go with the job like we guys did. Tike was breastfeeding Zon in the dining room. Afterward she'd once again run a wet rag over the tables, counters, and as much of the wall as she could reach. I didn't fault her for her light duty; it wasn't her calling.

At last I heard the engine start and the crunching gravel as Joe tore out of the parking lot. Tike and I were alone at last. She finished nursing Zon and put him to sleep in a corner before I heard her get back to scrubbing the walls and tables in the dining room. Like a maniac I tore into scouring the giant pots in the kitchen, determined to finish the thankless task and prove Joe wrong.

"Ron, could you please come here?" Tike's sweet voice called me from my pots to the front of the restaurant, so welcome to my ears after Joe's harsh tirade. Eager to help her, I ran to the front without rinsing my hands of the grease and detergent, the smell of which had filled my nostrils. In their place Tike's scent, a mixture of patchouli oil and coconut, refreshed me.

She wore a crooked smile, sexy as hell. Still, I was surprised when she grabbed me, pulling me tight to her chest and pressing her eager lips up against mine. Her hot tongue forced my lips and probed my mouth. I realized that I should have rinsed off before running over. I felt unclean, too dirty to touch her, and held my con- taminated hands away from her sublime body. She didn't care. Her crystal-blue eyes pleaded, hungry, welcoming me into their depths.

How could I resist? From the first day I'd longed for this moment with Tike, this beguiling Earth Mother, the embodiment of all I wanted in a woman. I needed to receive her healing love and to give her mine. Wordless, she let her body talk, caressing me, offering me the love and acceptance I craved with an ecstatic escape from the whirlwind of anger that was our master, Joe.

All I had to do was surrender, let her take charge and lead me to sublime happiness, but Joe's harsh words still reverberated in my brain, overriding my autonomous will. At any moment I expected him to come barging in, slamming his fists on the counter, bellowing that we've accomplished nothing, that the opening of our restaurant would be delayed, all due to *my* incompetence, my inability to do any goddamned thing right.

Still looking deep into her eyes, I gingerly took Tike's hands from my neck and told her, "I have to finish scouring those pots!"

Her eyes clouded over, perplexed, as I raced back to my drudge labor. It was terrible timing, I told myself. I'd make it up to her later, after I'd finished. That seemed to be a rational script. All my life's training had taught me to work harder, suck it up and prove myself to fathers, teachers, coaches, demanding authority figures, men who always wanted more and more and rarely praised what I gave.

Standing at the sink, the insanity of what I'd done hit me. Joe's work mania had colonized my brain; I'd become a cog in his *Modern Times* machine. Maybe I'd blown my best chance with Tike. Joe didn't even get back to check on our work. Too soon Jeff picked us up and brought us back to the ranch. I'd finished the pots but hadn't had a chance to rekindle the moment with Tike. Our work life had intervened, spoiling my best opportunity to make love to Tike.

Tike's poster had been prominently displayed by front door: *War is not healthy for children and other living things.* That hippie motto had become a ubiquitous part of the Peace Movement. On our return from the restaurant, Tike noticed it missing.

"Where's my poster, Joe?"

"That damn thing is too yin and also ugly. It clashes with the décor of the house."

"You mean you threw away my poster! You have no right to do that."

"I put it in the closet is all. The goddamn sentiments are too loud for me."

Tike raised her voice to Joe, lecturing him on keeping our priorities of peace and *make love not war* straight. It surprised me that he backed down. Tike hung her poster back in its place. She'd won a battle, but I didn't feel the issue was resolved.

We flopped around the living room and discussed our practical affairs—what needed doing on the land and to open our restaurant and how important food was—but none of them said anything about how anger was a corrosive force, especially as we were trying to build a society based on love, peace, and harmony. Being new, I thought it best to let the others lead the conversation, but as we discussed everything except anger, I began to realize they didn't feel able to confront Joe Sage, the source of it. This was more his than our place.

Things could change for the better around here, but it would take more yin, the female influence, to do it. We men were locked into a macho role of not admitting weakness, as doing so brought ridicule and contempt. We had to fake a brave front to each other, just as in the old society we'd dropped out of. When Joe wasn't around, we seemed to be calmer and have it together, but the house was more Joe's personal property than our shared living space. If we couldn't make the arrangement more mutual, I felt it wasn't a commune in the fullest sense. A little democracy would help.

JOANNE

IF IT HADN'T BEEN FOR the allure of Tike and Joanne, I'd have split the day after arriving, but there I remained. After three days sleeping nude in a free-love group marriage, it seemed remarkable, but I was still a virgin. To hell with that! I made up my mind to grab one of the ladies that night, but which of these two would be my first? I felt embarrassed by how I'd brushed off Tike and worried that she'd taken it personally. I needed a chance to explain myself in private and hadn't had the right moment. That left Joanne, who always slept beside Joe, like his main girl.

Although I'd seen Joe ball Tike, he rolled back to Joanne afterward. I was curious about whether Joanne felt neglected or relieved when he balled another woman right beside her. How emotionally involved was she with Joe? She'd had to stand up to Joe for her kid, and I wished I could have helped. I admired her guts as much as her beauty and wanted to bond with her as much as to satisfy my own sexual needs, which were, I felt certain, best done together.

Joanne showered and went to bed earlier than anyone else that night. The others were still in the living room, listening to Joe's electric piano renditions. Trying to be discreet, I held back a moment before coming into the bedroom, where I found Joanne on her side, cradling her head on her right elbow, her long, black hair cascading like a waterfall over her naked shoulders and back.

She'd pulled the sheet up over her trim midsection to right below her breasts. She may have intended to hide the stretch marks on her belly, but the sight of her voluptuous globes thrilled me, as if she'd put them on display to enchant me.

As relaxed as I could pretend to be, I began making small talk as I sat beside her and stripped off my clothes like it was the most natural thing in the world, which it was. Her tits jiggled when she laughed at one of my poor jokes. Naked, I lay down, face to face beside her. She seemed happy that I was there. Fierce emotions swirled inside of me: my desire for her and terror that I'd make a fool of myself. After all, I was in Joe's spot, but I couldn't betray my nervousness to this beautiful woman beside me. It would be my first time, but I had to act like a veteran of love. We gazed into each other's eyes. Her browns seemed warmer than they usually were, enflaming me with the reckless courage of love.

Not sure how else to proceed from small talk to sex, I shut up and let my fingers do the talking. Stroking her cheek, then down her neck to her shoulder I went, then along her arm and across to her breasts. Electricity shot through me at their warm touch. As I stroked her areolas, she moaned and put her arms around me. That beguiling moan was all the music I needed, enflaming me, arousing my still-untouched cock. I leaned over and kissed her lips, full and long, probing her hot mouth like Tike had mine such a short time ago. Joanne threw off the sheet, my cue to climb onto her. Her soft flesh radiated extreme heat that warmed my soul as much as my body.

After a brief exploration of my chest, her fingers seized my cock and directed it to her pussy, wet and ready. Entering her felt like coming home to where I belonged. She raised herself to meet my thrusts and then, with her reassuring, almost desperate words, half moaned, half whispered into my ear:

"Oh, yes, Ron, come on. Break me. Do it harder, harder, faster, yes, oh yes!"

With savage delight I rammed into her with ever more force. She was not a china doll, easily broken, but exactly the kind of woman I longed for, slamming herself back at me with equal force to my own.

JOANNE! She grunted and moaned under me, gripping me with her thighs, raking my back with her short, unpainted nails, encouraging my thrusts as if I could force my total self into her depths, ever deeper, merging my being into deeper union with her exotic otherness. She was the cosmic yin fulfillment of my yang. I held back, lasting long as I could until a whiteout dawn exploded in my brain as I shot my yang seed, my holy essence, into her.

Electric waves of pleasure rippled through me for some time after the glorious ride ended. We both lay still, contented. The warm thrill of being right where I belonged washed over me, and I didn't want to move off her body to any other spot, but it would have to end, as all things in this world must.

"How was it?" I had to ask. *Mmmm* was her contented answer. I wanted only to rest a moment and do it again and again. All the pornographic books and magazines I'd shoplifted over the years had advised me on foreplay techniques. I wanted to make an impression on Joanne, so I began nibbling her earlobes.

"Hey, man, what *are* you doing?" She giggled and pulled away to face me.

Did I go too far? "Oh, nothing, just playing around with you. Do you like to be tickled?"

"Not right now. Move over, you're too heavy." She rolled me onto where Joe slept.

"I'll be hard again soon. Okay?"

After a long moment she answered, "I'm going to the bathroom and check on things."

"Of course." I assumed she meant to look in on her son.

Throughout our lovemaking the door had opened and closed, people came and went, but we ignored them. Joe came in, looked around, then left without a word. He sometimes went to bed after everyone else, so I wasn't concerned. Jeff had told me we didn't have assigned sleeping spots. Beside me Tike got busy with Little Joe, so I put off making an immediate play for her too. Satisfied, I drifted into dreamland.

I woke as Joanne crawled back in beside me, smelling fresh and clean, inspiring an instant erection. I mounted her again, but she seemed to put in less and take out less pleasure in our second encounter. She must be tired, I thought. So I didn't hold back and let myself explode sooner to spare her. Finished, I rolled back over into contented slumber.

Maybe an hour later I came to as Joanne slipped back out. I heard her talking to Joe. Everything had to be all right because I felt so damn good. Then I wondered why Joe hadn't come to bed yet.

Had I done something wrong? I still wasn't sure how the system of sex worked around there. No one else seemed concerned; they were all fast asleep. If anyone besides Joe was getting any, it had to be while I was fast asleep.

Maybe Tike had told Joanne how I'd spurned her. Women talk to each other. Perhaps, out of a spirit of sisterhood, Joanne wanted me to make it right with Tike. That thought gave me a warm feeling of love toward both. It would be a taste of heaven to have them both crawl in beside me. I'd give them equal love. Whoever said a man cannot love more than one woman had it wrong. Their differences in personality and looks excited me beyond measure.

Maybe I'd been greedy, monopolizing Joanne so long, preventing another guy from getting his chance with her. That had to be the problem. I should have gone over to ball Tike and let Joe or Jeff get it on with Joanne. Maybe. However, it seemed uncouth to jump on Tike's luscious body as soon as I'd finished balling Joanne. Or was it? That's what Joe did my first night. We should all be talking about these things openly so each of us knew what was acceptable to the other. Maybe I ought to model myself after Joe and just pounce.

Fuck it. I was tired of fretting and pushed everything out of my mind. Although Joanne came and went all night long, I slept much better than usual the rest of the night.

MORNING AFTER

BEFORE BREAKFAST THE NEXT MORNING, I found Joe on the too-short sofa in the living room. He sat up, stretched his arms over his head, arched his back, then rose from the couch, confronting me with an insincere smile.

"Ron! Did you have a good night's sleep?"

Although his good cheer sounded phony, I stayed upbeat, unwilling to let him bring my excellent mood down. "Yeah, Joe, terrific! How about you?"

"I'm glad *you* slept because I sure as hell didn't! My goddamn back was killing me the whole goddamn night because I had to sleep on this fucking sofa."

"Too bad, man." I thought he was fishing for sympathy for his aging body and wasn't sure what else to say.

"Too bad?" He mimicked my words in a mocking voice. Then he blew up, shouting at me. "I had a hell of a night, and it's just too goddamn bad to you!"

"What the hell, Joe? Are you mad that I balled Joanne?" Maybe she was his property after all? The only thing I'd gleaned from *Stranger in a Strange Land* was that we had to share our love, free, without possessive ego getting in the way. Well, I'd watched Joe ball Tike. It was about time I got some too. Despite waiting days before breaking out of my virginity to prevent something like this from happening, I'd still run afoul of unwritten rules.

Joe's eyes got big, incredulous, and his tone softened. "No, of course not. We're all part of a family here. But didn't you notice anything different about the mattress?" He gave me a moment to think about it, then continued, "It's the only goddamn orthopedic mattress in the room! My back needs a hard surface, you know."

So that's it. I'd stayed on *his* special mattress without having the *decency* to shift to another one after I'd finished with Joanne. Although I'd noticed that it was harder than the others, I didn't think it was reserved for him. None of the mattresses were identical.

Joe had come in and out of the bedroom several times during the night. Asked if anything was wrong, he'd said, "Oh, nothing, nothing," and gone back out. Joe had few compunctions about speaking his mind. This sudden passivity was out of character.

"You should have said something to me, Joe. I'd have moved."

His jaw opened in mock shock, as if he'd never thought of that. "You're right, but I didn't want to interfere with you getting your rocks off balling Joanne. She came out to check on how I was doing but *you* never did."

Joe worried about spoiling *my* night? That seemed ridiculous. He could explode in rage for any reason, but he'd suffered in silence all night, only to tell me off in the morning. It was obvious that we needed better communication and understanding among ourselves if we were going to be close. We all got naked and slept in the same room but still needed to talk more to each other if we were to build a more loving, non-monogamous family.

Joe was our linchpin. I gave him credit; he'd set up and financed our dream society. He laid down the rules, therefore it had turned into a patriarchy, which still could have worked if he didn't raise a fuss and get upset all the time. His outbursts put us all on edge. Maybe his reluctance to spoil my night with Joanne was a good sign. He was trying to restrain himself.

I'd left one angry father at home and didn't need any more nerve-wracking drama in my life. We'd all come together to create a society of free love and peace. That took more focused effort than we'd given it yet.

Jeff was one level-headed dude I could open up to without acrimony. Talking to him refreshed me and took the edge off Joe's temper tantrums. Later that day I admitted to him that Joanne had been my first-time lover.

"Really, your first fuck? Well, congratulations, man!" He clapped me on my back.

Finding myself alone with Joanne in a rare moment of leisure, she asked me if I'd ever had a dog and what his name was.

"Sure, I had a beagle named Tippy."

"Tippy!" She raised her voice in exasperation. "That's a *square* name, not very original."

"No, but I'd only been nine years old when we got him."

Maybe she missed a mutt of her own? She seemed even more preoccupied than usual, and I wondered if I had anything to do with it. I asked her about her kid, whether he missed his dad or was happier here than there and whether Joe was nicer to him since she'd confronted him. It was just small talk, but I also wanted her to see whether we could stand together to create a common front. We wouldn't have to put up with Joe's shit if we laid it on the line all together.

Joanne said that her Chinese old man wasn't any better than Joe at keeping a cool head. He'd been calling her. I'd watched her sphinxlike face as she held the receiver to her ear, saying little beyond *uh-huh* as she listened to his pleading. He wanted her back. Who could blame him? Beyond being the mother of his child, Joanne was gorgeous, imbued with erotic charm. Sharing her in this group marriage was one thing, but I didn't want to lose her to distant California. After she hung up, I asked her, "Will you go back to him?"

"I don't know. It depends." She brushed me off, leaving me unsure.

"At least here you have more than one guy to take care of you. Right?" I nudged her and winked. "That's got to be better than just one crabby jerk of a husband."

She laughed at that and I gave her a quick kiss before I had to get back to whichever job I'd been assigned that day.

In my theory of matrimony, monogamy was too narrow, stingy, and limited for true happiness. The more the merrier. I'd always wanted a harem, but I saw no reason to be selfish and keep all the women to myself alone. When I'd read about polyandry, the marriage of a woman with more than one mate, it seemed the perfect combination, a mutual harem in the form of a group marriage. Joe Sage's family was on the right track.

111

People said you couldn't love more than one person, or else they differentiate between love and lust, denigrating the latter, forcing errant husbands to beg whichever lover got upset to forgive their indiscretions. But that missed the point. True love had to be wide, not narrow. Each person has different aspects to share, so, by a wider love, we could learn to open our hearts up and appreciate the complexity and individuality of each mate. In our family we were supposed to share like that. It wasn't perfect yet, but I was an optimist and hoped we could work on it.

LOVE'S LOSS

THE SEVEN PATHS WASN'T OFFICIALLY open yet, but we served simple meals to the few brave souls who ventured in. Joe was aware that he had to educate people by trying it out first. A trio of wild-eyed longhairs trooped in, stoned out of their gourds and talking in a strange invented lingo known only to themselves. One of the men wore a see-through, plastic shower curtain someone had sewn together into a short robe that only reached his emaciated knees and elbows, his hairy body on display. Another of them bragged to me of shootouts with a rival band of hippies who had purloined some of their supplies. They all smelled of stale sweat, cheap wine, and smoky campfires, which they proclaimed to all within hearing equaled freedom. Few such customers could come up with the price of a coffee at another establishment, and we offered them Mu tea for free, but even these poor specimens of the counterculture found the lack of sweetener a deal-breaker and stormed out.

True, the taste had to be acquired. Almost everyone found macrobiotic food bland, which it was. Only a select few ecology-minded souls ventured in and were pleased with our fare. We were still busy stocking up for an official grand opening once Joe was satisfied with its purity.

Few of the local hipsters I saw wandering the streets of Taos were as clean as we were. Without convenient running water it was hard to be too concerned with hygiene. I worried about the dirt-encrusted children. They were as poor as they looked, often carried papoose style by harried mothers. What they all had was an arrogant confidence in their free, unencumbered lifestyle. It was a relief to see people less structured than we in Joe Sage's family were beginning to

113

be, but I wasn't impressed with the local hippies as examples I wanted to emulate.

Little Joe and Tike were intertwined in deep sleep that I wouldn't disturb, but Joanne stayed up in the living room talking with Joe after the rest of us retired. Their conversation began to sound like a rambling argument. I wanted to go out there and asked Jeff to join me.

"I think Joanne could use some moral support," I said. "Shouldn't we make this a family thing?"

"They don't need interference from us," Jeff insisted. "Everything will work itself out by morning."

Maybe Jeff, older and wiser, was right. Joe's voice sounded soft and pleading with her, not as forceful as the way he spoke to the men. Joanne's beautiful yin power brought his manic yang down a few notches. I returned to my original mattress at the end rather than trigger any more trip wires. Maybe Joanne would come to me on her own that night. Tomorrow's clear light would give us a better perspective on things, I thought as I drifted into sleep.

At dawn I awoke to find Joe alone on his firm mattress. I sought Joanne, finding her in the extra bedroom with her son. She refused to fill me in. She didn't join us over breakfast but stayed with her boy in the back bedroom. Joe made an announcement.

"Joanne's decided to split back to her old man in California."

His flippant words tried to take the edge off the uncomfortable situation, but it shocked me out of my usual good morning spirits. She was my first lover. I—we—were losing one of our only two women, a lover and companion to each of us. The atmosphere become oppressive with all our unspoken feelings. *Why?*

"She's made up her mind," Joe said, flinging his hand at the ceiling with exasperation. "I couldn't convince her to stay. She'll see her mistake and come back to us."

Then he rolled onto the next item on the agenda. "Who's going to the restaurant?" Joe turned to me. "Ron, you stick around to work on the ranch. Jeff will swing back later, and you guys can string up the fence."

Joe had ordered a shipment of live pheasants. Despite what some people thought, macrobiotics was not a vegetarian concept. Pheasants were a yang food item, and we had to build a tight enclosure for them.

After sending everyone else off, Joe put his arm around my shoulder, something he'd never done before, and spoke in a reasonable voice of concern. "Ron, you go rap with her. Maybe you can change her mind."

Joanne was packing her suitcase in the bedroom with her son sleeping beside her. She glanced up and asked, "Ron, could you help me here?"

"Sure." I helped her latch her two large suitcases, full of stylish clothing, which took my full weight to close tight.

"I already called a taxi," she said, attempting a cheerful voice that sounded forced. "It should arrive in half an hour to take us to the airport."

It made me glad we were far enough out in the boonies to delay the cab. I wanted more precious time with her. My throat felt tight. It was difficult for me to speak, but I struggled to say something, hoping to change her mind. How should I express my feelings in this situation without inciting her contempt and rejection?

"You know I'll be sorry to see you go, all of us will."

"I know." She didn't look at me but brushed her fingers through her son's bushy head. "My husband sent us a ticket. He wants us back and, well, he's my husband, my boy's father."

Failing to find the right words of comfort, I tried to console her with a hug. She shrugged me off.

"Not now, I don't feel like it." Her eyes, red from crying, stared up into mine like cold stones. She'd flushed out her emotions with her tears. All that remained was her resolve to leave our family and return to her renegotiated marriage. She must have gotten her despised husband to come around to her side for her to go back.

I wanted to scream but only whimpered. *What about us? Forget about Joe!* Of course, I meant *us* in the communal sense, true to our commitment to utopian shared love. I didn't want to be selfish or square in her eyes, but I feared voicing my feelings would sound so pathetic, as had the name of my dog. Was I too square for a hip chick like herself?

Joanne had been my first sexual partner. I loved her and wanted more from her, some acknowledgement of our recent passion, but standing beside her, I felt I'd become a mere shadow, an inconsequential stranger to her, as if I'd never pumped my yang life force deep into her yin, her embracing womb. A part of me wanted to seize her, force myself upon her, remind her of what we, for such a brief moment in time, had. But no, I had to be cool, not act like the brute caveman I wanted to be. My yang had to be reined in, controlled.

She was going back to a husband she'd escaped and told me she hated. But what about us? Was there ever an *us* anyway? Weren't we all, men and women, alone, mere isolates, sharing the same space but connecting only in brief moments of passion that meant something different, depending on the primal needs of each of us at the time? Everyone we cared about, I knew, was fated to leave us; transience was the hard reality that had to be accepted. The juice of life could only be savored in brief moments.

Honk, honk! The taxi was outside the gate. Lugging her two oversize suitcases, I walked her out and hoisted her belongings into the trunk. She didn't offer me a kiss even then but finally a warm hug, all too brief, and what I took as a meaningful glance as she slid with her still-sleeping son into the back seat. I took what comfort I could from that look that could have meant little or nothing. She didn't look back as the driver stepped on the gas and disappeared around the bend. Maybe we'd built a karmic connection. Maybe someday, either here or elsewhere, a millennium away on the vast horizon, we'd renew all the passion I already missed.

Time may not heal but it moves us along. Jeff got back from the restaurant. We gathered our tools in the shed. Using the posthole digger, we sank a few more holes to those that he'd dug earlier in the week, tamped in all the posts with the butts of our shovels, and nailed the wire to the first post. Then we hooked up the come-along to pull the mesh tight to the next one. I'd done this work with my dad and knew it well. Working with Jeff was a pleasure; we made a good team. A huge relief after my nightmare workday with Joe.

About halfway through the job, we saw a couple of dudes coming from a long way off. They looked like beatniks, in black clothes with shoulder-length hair, coming down the valley toward us. As they got closer, I saw they had earrings and bits of turquoise jewelry decorating their wrists and clothes.

"Hey, man," they called out to us, and we waved them over, glad for a rest and a chat. They arrived on the other side of the fence. One of them had a leather pouch hung around his neck. He took something from it and held it out to us. "Ever seen one of these before?"

It looked like a shining, little black cross, less than two inches across, almost like the Maltese crosses that were so popular in my high school, or the German Iron Cross from the World Wars, except that this appeared to be natural. He passed it through the fence to us and took out more.

"These are Apache Tears, man. Ever heard about them?"

"Yeah," Jeff said. "I used to collect rocks. They're obsidian, volcanic rock, a kind of natural glass."

"Well, ya know, Apache Tears are a powerful protection from negative forces. Do you believe in magic?"

Jeff and I nodded our heads yes.

"Yeah, sure," his friend added. "Magic is all around us, man, especially in this enchanted country. That's what pulled us here to this colorful land."

"Me too," I added.

The one with the gems recounted the legend. "The Apaches fought long and hard against the White Eyes—that's what they called us, you know. In one battle the cavalry had a bunch of their warriors trapped, surrounded on a mountain. Instead of surrendering, the Apaches rode their horses off a cliff to their deaths. The tears of their wives and children turned into these stones when they hit the ground. Spooky, huh?"

"I dunno, man," the other one said. "That's a crazy, far-out story, but I do think those rocks have energy. Gives me a feel-good vibe seeing or touching them."

"We're herding goats for this old Indian woman," the first one said. "She lives way up there in the mountains." With a vague wave of his hand, he indicated a northwest direction. "It's sacred ground up there, ancient campsites where we found the Tears, man, also arrowheads and broken pottery like this." He pulled a shard out of his bag; the stylized figure of a humpbacked flute player adorned the rounded exterior. "This one's special. Most only have geometric decorations on 'em."

His friend passed a chipped piece through the fence to me. "Here, man, take it, we got plenty. Put it under your pillow when you sleep. In your dreams you'll tune in on the spirt songs of ancient warriors. These hills, man, are full of powerful Indian spirits."

The relaxed attitude of these free-spirited herders filled me with envy. Maybe it was their pastoral job, which had always appealed to me. Herding animals necessitated understanding them. That produced more empathy in a person than grubbing in the dirt to coax plants to grow. Somehow, we all had to make a living, find nourishment, and still feel good about ourselves. We shouldn't have to abuse each other just to survive in this world.

Joe's angry words still rang in my ears. Part of me wanted to drop everything and join these herders, but I couldn't abandon the others, especially Tike. I felt a deep connection to everyone except Joe. For him I had a mix of admiration and disapproval bordering on anger, complicated feelings. He'd taken me into his world, and I was grateful, but things had to improve or our little society, based on the promise of love, would disintegrate. I didn't want that. We were the vanguard and had to succeed to usher in a new style of living on this violent planet.

CHARLIE'S ANGELS

TWO NEW GIRLS BLEW IN from California late one night. After losing Joanne, Tike had been our only *wife* to four theoretical husbands, not that I saw her being overwhelmed. Maybe Tike and Little Joe were getting it on at the restaurant. Working as hard as we did every day, we zonked out as soon as we hit the sheets, and I never witnessed Jeff get any action at all, a sad state of affairs.

The new girls almost equalized our boy-girl ratio, but neither of them would win a beauty prize or could ever replace Joanne. Joe didn't seem pleased with either of them.

One was bony, stoop-shouldered, and hollow-chested. Life seemed to have dealt her a bad hand, leaving her with a bitter, argumentative personality as thorny as a cactus. Uninterested in her sexually, I felt pity for her and never even learned her name.

The other was Leslie, a fleshier brunette, although not as appealing as Joanne had been. Compared to her friend, however, she was ravishing, with a medium-sized bosom. She sidled up beside me on her first morning during breakfast. Still smarting from the loss of Joanne, I focused on my bland oatmeal and, trying not to be rude, accepted her presence with equanimity.

"You know, Ron, I'm a trained masseuse. I could give you a full-body massage right after breakfast if you like."

"Okay, that sounds good to me." That cheered me a little from my lovesick doldrums.

Joe, trying to marshal his forces for a productive day, gave me an evil look so I spoke up.

"It's okay, Joe. How about I do house duty this morning?" Someone always needed to be around the ranch to keep an eye on things.

"Okay?" he said with more sarcasm than conviction in his voice. "Yeah, far out, I guess that's cool by me."

Taking my hand, Leslie asked, "Can we go somewhere for a little privacy?" I took her into the other bedroom, where Joanne had waited for her cab and deliverance from our family.

"What's the big fucking deal with him anyway?" She meant Joe, of course, having noticed how he spoke to me.

"He's a moody character. I've given up trying to figure him out."

"He wanted to fuck me last night, just grabbed me and said, 'Let's ball.' We hadn't even talked yet, jeez, but I told him I wasn't in the fucking mood."

Maybe that explained her sudden interest in me, to keep Joe off her back.

"Christ, I was tired, ya know, Ron, hitching in from the California desert. Charlie, the guy we were staying with, told us to go stay with Joe Sage a while. So here we are."

There were two single mattresses on the floor, others stacked in the large closet. Under Leslie's direction and with her eager help, I stripped off my clothes and lay face-down while she took off her top and jeans, leaving her panties on. Leslie warmed scented oil in her hands before applying it to my back, soothing me despite the nagging crap Joe put in my head.

Joe had a knack for saying things that got under my skin, making me feel less than worthy. We were always walking on eggshells around him, but he claimed to be a holy man, a master of occult arts. I'd read as much as I could find about Tantra, the difficult lightning path to spiritual illumination. Guru yoga, devotion to a master, was the key to spiritual success. Did I owe this *Sage* named Joe a guru's devotion or was that misplaced loyalty?

Milarepa, the famous Tibetan yogi, had attained Buddhahood in one lifetime by enduring the abuse and overwhelming tasks that his guru, Marpa, imposed on him. Was Joe my Marpa or simply a power-drunk dictator? How can you tell the difference ahead of time between a dictator and an empowered guru like Marpa? I was conflicted about devoting myself to any flawed individual. Joe's loud ranting and humiliation of me, of all of us, may have been his skillful means to destroy our egos so we could achieve spiritual results, but I wasn't sure if that was enough justification.

My nagging thoughts dissipated as I surrendered to Leslie's soothing hands. As her hands kneaded my flesh, her incessant drone of conversation, like a waterfall of words, soothed my mind, eroding Joe from my brain. This was my first naked body massage, and I'd become an instant fan.

"Turn over," Leslie commanded. She continued kneading, working her way up from each joint of my fingers to my palms, arms, and shoulders, then from my toes to my calves and thighs, her mouth going a mile a minute as she worked, lulling me into relaxation.

She told me about the Haight-Asbury scene and how it differed from the streets in Hollywood and the City of Angels—Los Angeles, where she was from. She reached my chest, working her way with sultry languor to my abdomen as she informed me that men pay a lot of money for what she was doing for me now free of charge.

"Uh-huh," I mumbled at what I assumed were appropriate times, when I felt she expected a response. I didn't feel like having a full-blown conversation right then. My thoughts and feelings were too jumbled to express. Would she appreciate my thoughts on Milarepa? There was no need to bother her with that.

Joanne and Tike were both on my mind too. Although I'd rather be with either of them, I relaxed to enjoy pure pleasure with Leslie. Did a woman have to be a classic beauty to satisfy me? Was I a cad to think of other girls while enjoying this one? *That was then, this is now*, I told myself. Love was mercy; it behooved me to love the one with me in the here and now rather than the ghost memory of the departed. Every woman needed loving as much as every man, and I resolved to be a man and open my body and heart to Leslie.

With a half-mast erection, I'd become passive putty in her hands, letting her do all the work. She moved her hands around my belly, closer and closer to the root of my being. My rod, my staff, she comforted with a squeeze and a tug, so nonchalant, almost as an afterthought. The thought of her taking the initiative, seducing me, *getting me off* while I lay there like a pasha, turned me on. My cock jumped to full erection with eager expectation, happy in her warm, wet hands. For one electric moment I thought she would jerk me off or give me a blow job, something I'd heard so much about, but then she released her grip on me.

"Too bad, Ron. I'm tired right now." She gave my cock a last squeeze and, *splat*, slapped it back against my belly. "Get dressed, I'm done for now."

She had to be joking. My joystick stood, rock-hard and ready, but no, she put her top on and sat on the mattress across from me. Although disappointed, I didn't press her. *Fuck it.* I felt too relaxed and it seemed beneath me to beg. *She's not my type*, I told myself again, even though I knew every woman could be my type in the right circumstances, but she had to want it too. Maybe we'd fuck later, after she rested. I'd let her call the shots. It seemed we were *buddies* now, which is not always a path to sex in a woman's mind.

Leslie continued rambling on about her California life while I only half listened. She told me about a mysterious group she stayed with in Death Valley in the California desert. They also called themselves The Family, just as we did. It was an unremarkable label. The leader, head of that family, they called *The Son of Man*. That's when my interest pricked up.

"Is it a Christian trip? Why else would they use that term? Jesus never called himself the Son of God, only the Son of man."

"Maybe so," she said, "but The Family is more into witchcraft than some fundamentalist Christian bullshit. The dude's real name is Charlie Manson, get it? *Man-son*, Son of Man. Pretty crafty, huh?"

"Yeah, that's far out," I said with a touch of sarcasm. "Just a play on words, huh?" In my mind I dismissed it as only another trippy fantasy.

"They're into a really *heavy* trip, though."

"What do you mean by heavy?"

"A real power trip. I bet you'd like it there. They have dune buggies and ride around the desert playing war games, preparing for the Apocalypse. Charlie says it will be a race war, the blacks will rise up and destroy this country, but then Charlie, with his superior mind, will take over. He's kind of a racist, thinks blacks are all bugaboos." She laughed and rocked back on the mattress. "I think they've a lot of negative energy because they eat *way* too much meat."

Not all hippies, I was learning, were free of prejudice. Leslie had bought into the common assumption of vegetarian food fetishists that eating meat caused a person to become violent and aggressive. That didn't ring true to me; I knew Hitler was a vegetarian. Since I'd been with Joe, we hadn't eaten any meat, and there was way too much nasty, angry shouting going on around here, at least from Joe. How negative could these Manson people be? I wondered.

Later that morning I answered a knock at the door. The guy was short, a little over five feet, and dark-complexioned, with a compact frame. His medium-length, shaggy black hair and beard framed a hard face with piercing black eyes. They stared into mine with ice-cold malevolence, chilling me. He was laying a head trip on me, trying to intimidate me. Instinctively I drew back, even though I knew I shouldn't flinch from a guy like that. I'd gotten this treatment from toughs back in the neighborhood. Relaxed from my massage, he'd caught me off guard and I felt vulnerable. The vibe the dude gave off assured me that he was capable of anything, maybe even murder. My hands oozed sweat and my mind stumbled into a fight-or-flight mode. Was this stranger one of the anti-hippie Chicanos? He didn't seem Hispanic, despite his complexion. We were headed for trouble in Taos, and I thought we ought to get guns to be prepared for it, but Joe said the local hostility was exaggerated. Our spiritual vibes were all the firepower we needed.

Putting on a fake brave front, I extended my hand, jabbering a "How're ya doing, man?" When he didn't react, I asked, "Hey, man, what's happening?" He refused my hand. I felt like I was just sputtering gibberish, which didn't lighten his threatening demeanor. Never taking his eyes off me, which were like two drills boring into my skull, he asked *where the fuck* Joe was.

"Which Joe do you mean?"

"Sage," he snarled.

I wondered if I should tell him. Maybe he was a hit man, sent by Joe's Good Karma business partners back in California, but from what I could see, he didn't seem to be packing heat in his embroidered shirt and jeans.

"Joe Sage should be back from the restaurant soon, man. Wanna wait?"

"No, I goddamn don't," he spat the words at me.

Hoping to defuse the tension, I asked him who he was and where he was from, but he stared me down with contempt.

"Oh, I'll be back," he said, still fixing me with his withering stare. Then the mysterious stranger asked me a bizarre question. "Did you ever live with *Negroes* or have much to do with them?"

The way he stretched out the word "Negroes" cued me to his dislike of them. What was his trip? I said no, I hadn't had the opportunity to get to know any blacks. His indelicate gaze continued probing my soul, causing my panic to rise in my throat as I forced myself to stare back, with my own jangled concentration, into his hard eyes. A wicked sneer crossed his face. Dripping with sarcasm, he said: "I bet you'd get along really well with them Negroes."

It didn't seem intended as a compliment. Saying nothing more, I shut the door. He'd never given me his name, and I never saw the satanic-looking dude again.

Later that year, after the Charles Manson murders splashed across the headlines, I had a sense of having heard his name and seen his mug before. After a while it hit me: Manson, the Son of Man! Those demonic eyes on the television reminded me of the mysterious visitor. I can't be certain that the guy I met was *the* Charles Manson, but if he wasn't, it was his evil twin.

Charles Manson was only one of too many dangerous sociopaths loose on the American landscape. Many of them passed through Taos, where the action was supposed to be.

Years later, reading *Helter Skelter* by Vincent Bugliosi, I saw Joe Sage mentioned as an acquaintance of the Manson Family. Linda Kasabian, of Manson's harem, escaped his clutches by running to Joe's Ranch after the murders that summer. She told Joe about them, but he didn't believe her. Joe telephoned Manson, who told him Linda was tripping, and her ego needed to die.

In retrospect I wonder if Manson sent his girls to scout Joe's place for some nefarious plan.

BREAKING BREAD

THE SCRAWNY CALIFORNIA GIRL HAD a big box of Sun-Maid Golden Raisins and donated them to our larder. We'd been eating black raisins every morning in our oatmeal. Most of us assumed those golden raisins would be all right too. Joe was out while the rest of us were at the restaurant, and Tike decided to bake up a supply of raisin bread. Looking for ingredients, she discovered that we were out of the black ones. We'd use the golden.

We all jumped in, eager to help. Sharing work was one of the terrific things about communal life. It seemed more like play as we pitched in with gusto to knead and shape the dough, letting it rise in deep bread pans. After baking, twelve loaves were lined up to cool along the counter in the kitchen. We cut into one; it was delicious! Then we awaited Joe, confident of his praise, certain our effort would please him.

The aroma of our fresh-baked bread filled the restaurant with a warm, joyous smell that made everyone salivate. Joe beamed with good vibes when he bounced in. "It tastes great," he proclaimed, munching on a thick slice, but after he'd taken another bite, he noticed that the raisins weren't black. "Where did we get these god-damn raisins?"

"The new girl brought them as her contribution," Tike explained, apprehension in her voice. "Fortunate, too, because we were out of the black ones. It was the perfect amount, we stretched it to make twelve loaves."

"Where's the package?" Joe asked, his voice icy. It was in the garbage barrel, but he dug under some food refuse and found it. "Sun-Maid Golden Raisins," he read aloud.

It was a well-known brand, considered good quality food in most households, but it raised alarm bells in Joe's mind. How could this commercial brand be chemical free, pure enough for our diet? Sure enough, he found an additive, sulfur dioxide. He threw a fit.

"This goddamn shit doesn't belong here!" Joe's voice rose as he crumpled the box into a ball and slam-dunked it back into the garbage where he said it belonged. Once again, he had become the dark-faced demon of our nightmares. He grabbed one loaf of cooling bread after another and threw them with a sickening thud into the garbage can with whatever disgusting crud was already there.

The sight deflated me. What an awful waste of delicious food. After all our harmonious work, I couldn't believe that he'd throw away the entire batch over a few trace chemicals. We probably got that much of a dose from the air we breathed. There were plenty of hungry hippies in town like the hog farmers, who scrounged food from dumpsters for free feeds. They'd devour this bread with relish. All my life I despised waste, and this was egregious. I considered salvaging some of it when Joe was gone but didn't have a chance. Maybe some dumpster-diving hippies found them later. I'd like to think so, otherwise the worms ate well.

The workday was ended, time to load up and go back to the ranch. Little Joe and Tike looked resigned and said not a word as they trudged to the van. Our spirits had been crushed. The new girls were especially crestfallen as it was their offering that had caused such a stir. It was a dark day in our nascent family, and I reassessed the wisdom of remaining.

"How could you *all* be so goddamn stupid!" our Sage wanted to know when we got back that evening. After all his lectures and George Oshawa readings, it was obvious that none of us understood what was wholesome and what was toxic and impure.

There were some things I liked about a macrobiotic diet. Brown rice was great. I'd long eaten it and other whole grains when I could. It was true about not needing toilet paper; my shit was firm and regular and left no visible residue. But the philosophy behind macrobiotics was too narrow and simplistic to me. I kept that opinion to myself, of course, knowing that Joe would only shout it down. There was enough angry discourse without my adding to it. I couldn't, however, accept the dualistic yin-yang philosophy. It was too fanatical and arbitrary in categorizing food. I'd already accepted the logic of Edgar Cayce's system: drink lots of water, less meat, more whole grains, fresh fruits and vegetables, brown rice too. That made sense, but ultimately, I felt food was only part of the equation. What good was a clean regimen of healthy food if we screamed abuse at each other and wallowed in negative energy?

Joe's anger was a far more potent danger to us than a little too much yin in our diet or even a few chemicals.

VISITATIONS

I WAS ALONE AT THE restaurant when an old Indian with the usual long braided hair came in. Speaking in slow and uncertain English, he asked if we'd buy some of his beans and other products of his land. I wanted to say yes. Here was a mellow-tempered fellow who appeared to be in harmony with himself and his surroundings. But the scene Joe raised the day before over impure ingredients was still too fresh in my mind. I promised the old man I'd talk to our Sage but told him I doubted if he'd want to buy the local produce. After all, it wasn't Japanese! As he turned away, crestfallen, I felt that I'd ruined the old man's day, which sent me into a glum emotional tailspin. If it was only up to me, I'd buy his stuff.

He'd been gone only a little while when a car screeched to halt, raising a cloud of dust outside. A trio of young Chicano men trooped in. Their vibe was altogether different from my last visitor. These hombres looked like trouble. Shouting and laughing in Spanish, they kicked chairs out of their way and plopped their cowboy boots up on tables as they took over a corner of the empty restaurant. The way these devil-may-care young thugs flaunted their contempt of me, and this hippie establishment reminded me of the sneering banditos in old Westerns.

I felt like a bartender in the Westerns: *I don't want no trouble here, amigos.* I was supposed to be in charge but alone and vulnerable. I hid my fear under the smile I plastered on my face. Greeting them with a *Buenos días,* I showed them our menu, hoping to mollify them.

We were only serving a few ready-made items, like sesame balls, brown rice, and adzuki beans, which were kept in a warmer, or I could whip up a couple of soy burgers from the batter sitting in the fridge. The Chicanos insisted on speaking only Spanish to me, which I hadn't gotten a grip on beyond *hello* and *goodbye*. They must have been insulting me by the way one of them laughed like a hyena every time his friend spoke to me. I swallowed my pride and ignored the obvious, worried that they might smash up the place if given half an excuse.

"Try some of these." I offered sample sesame balls free of charge.

The lean one, who seemed to be the leader, took a bite and then spit it on the floor.

"What's this shit, *pendejo*? This *pinche* crap is fucking garbage!" He made a face. "Are you trying to poison me, *ese*?" The others laughed, challenging me to do something about it.

It would be stupid to take them on. I'd get my ass stomped, and they'd smash up the place. Although seething inside I kept an outward calm, doing my best to be straight with these guys, no bullshit.

"The food is new to me too, man, but it's supposed to be healthy. If you don't like it, okay, a lot of people don't. I'm not too crazy about it either. Try some of this Mu tea."

None of them were happy about that either, but by the time Jeff came back, my *friends* had settled down a bit and even tried a few more samples. Jeff asked me if they'd paid for anything. They hadn't but he wasn't in a mood to confront them either.

When Joe Sage walked in, the Chicanos suddenly got up and left. As they sauntered out the double doors, I couldn't help thinking that they'd been casing the joint. Joe watched them leave with concern.

"What the fuck did those guys want? They give you any trouble?"

"Just a hard time and they spit the samples I gave them on the floor."

"Well, clean it up, goddamn it."

"Yeah, Joe, I was about to."

We would have more trouble with these rambunctious toughs, I felt that in my bones.

I remembered the old Indian trying to sell his produce and told Joe.

"What's his name?" Joe seemed interested; I hadn't expected that.

"I didn't get it." Then, to cover my ass, I added, "I didn't think you'd want that stuff. How do we know if it's macrobiotic or organic?"

"You didn't think I'd want it?" Joe's words dripped with sarcasm, and he stepped back, wide-eyed in mock amazement. "The goddamn stuff these farmers grow around here is pure organic, they can't afford any goddamn chemicals!" Joe started to get upset, but this time he caught himself. "Well, maybe I know the guy." He started talking to himself under his breath as he walked away.

Later, back at the ranch, more shouting disturbed our peace. Joe began picking on Leslie's companion, the other California girl, saying that she was a good-for-nothing lazy bitch, a bad influence on our tidy little family. She defied him, screaming, *I am not*, which caused Joe to explode, shrieking at her.

"Why the hell don't you go ahead and leave us then? Go on, get the fuck out of here!"

All of us were shocked into silence. We hadn't bonded with her yet, but I felt sympathetic. She wasn't pretty or witty, and it was obvious Joe didn't want to ball her, but it seemed cruel, a crime to treat her that way.

"Go ahead, get the *fuck* out and leave us if you want, goddamn it, I don't care. This place is for people who show the right stuff, work hard and can stick it out!" Joe had the final word. She shut up and sulked but didn't leave. Maybe she had nowhere else to go.

Joe stomped around the living room, lecturing and bragging about all he'd done for the hippie community in Taos. He'd helped start the free clinic and a telephone help line for kids in crisis. Cool, but I wondered where his compassion or simple consideration was for each of us who slaved for him. How could he be surprised that Joanne left after the way he'd treated her little son?

We were being molded into mere lackeys, working for Joe, not for our common interest. I could've dug supporting his family if I'd been given a real stake in it, but I didn't feel this was *my* family or even *our* family; it was *his* family and it was Joe's way or the highway. It wasn't much different than what I'd had to put up with at home, but I'd stay for Tike's sake.

CULTURE CLASH

"THEY'RE SHOOTING AT ME! THE Mexicans are trying to kill me!" Like a wild-eyed Paul Revere, an out-of-breath Jeff barged in the back door from the fields.

It was about nine in the evening, still light outside, on Thursday, May fifteenth. The grand opening of the Seven Paths Restaurant was scheduled for the next day. Joe Sage and I had been alone at the ranch, waiting for the others to get back in the living room. Tike and Little Joe, ever the consummate artists, had stayed behind for some last-minute touch-ups to their painted-window masterpiece while Jeff ran a few errands.

When he caught his breath, Jeff elaborated. A car tried to run his van off the road as soon as he left the restaurant. He stepped on the gas, and they chased him all the way from Taos. The mysterious car caught up to him after Jeff made the turn onto Rancho de Taos. Careening in front, it forced him onto the shoulder.

Bang, bang, bang! They fired several shots, a couple of which hit the van. Jeff didn't wait around to see how accurate their shooting was.

"Fuck no! Let them use the van for target practice for all I care," he said, still shaking. "I don't need to get my ass shot off!"

Then the phone rang. Joe grabbed the receiver, but an excited voice on the other end didn't give him a chance to speak for a long minute. Finally, he spoke.

"Okay, I'll call the cops. Be careful, take care of Tike."

After he hung up, Joe slumped into the chair, open-mouthed and dazed as if shocked. He let out a long sigh and filled us in.

"That was Little Joe. He said a gang of rowdy Chicanos attacked the restaurant, smashing up all the goddamn windows. He and Tike ran for it, they're okay, but he doesn't know how bad the damage to the restaurant is."

The phone rang again. We learned there had been simultaneous attacks on hippie establishments all over Taos; it looked like a coordinated offensive by an anti-hippie group.

It sounded like the amazing artwork that Little Joe and Tike had put so much of their time and artistic souls into was gone. Maybe the whole restaurant had been damaged. We'd have to delay the grand opening for sure.

My thoughts ran to how easily our grand schemes can be dashed to bits. That seemed to be the message of Navajo and Tibetan sand paintings, or mandalas, created to convey a sacred truth, like Tike's astrological art, only to be destroyed, returned to the natural order of chaos after the ceremony.

"What should we do now, Joe?" Jeff stared at him, expectant, waiting for direction.

Joe said nothing. He hadn't expected this scale of reaction from the anti-hippie Chicanos. Joe claimed to be an Indian and had become a well-entrenched local, an economic asset to the community, not one of us newcomer hippies, but he was committed to New Age philosophies, and his unconventional family and business went against the conservative Catholic culture. Unlike Joe, I'd been expecting the underlying resentment to blow up and almost felt relieved that it had started.

It would be up to us to react. Young and excited by this dramatic turn of events, I wanted to jump into action. Too long I'd endured Joe's anger and blame. I needed a catharsis to clear the awful stress from my mind. This seemed to be a brave new adventure in the Old West.

"They'll never leave us alone unless we stand up to them," I said. "The only thing that bullies respect is reckless courage."

"They might be still out there, goddamn it." Joe stared at me, a dumbfounded look still on his leathery face. "You want to go? Go ahead."

"Good. If they're out there, maybe we can get their license number."

It sounded crazy, but I knew they expected scared hippies to run away. Maybe it would shock them if we made a stand. Of course, I'd been inspired by too many war books. A crazy exhilaration took hold of me.

"Come on, Jeff! *Hoka hey!*" I shouted the Sioux war cry that resounded in my brain like a trumpet call. "It's a goddamn good day to die today."

I continued to shout exultant war cries. It felt so *goddamn* good to shout and run into the fray, come what may. A wave of gratitude even washed through me that these enemies of ours gave us the opportunity for some active drama that didn't involve yelling at each other. Maybe now Joe could realize how much we meant to him, how much he owed us for all we did and put up with.

I ran out the back, across our irrigated fields. The plants were bigger and greener than that miserable day when I couldn't keep up with Joe. Jeff came running after me but kept some distance behind. The Chicanos were gone. If they'd lingered, they could have filled us with lead if they wanted to. Jeff and I had not a gun nor a knife between us. The van sat, looking forlorn, on the shoulder of the empty highway, its driver's side door wide open the way Jeff left it.

We found cracks in the windshield, already spiderwebbing out from where a couple projectiles had hit. There had been no theft nor any other damage to the vehicle. Joe finally came out too and said that the police were on their way. Jeff and I waited by the road to talk to the policeman while Joe drove his car into town to check on the restaurant.

The officer from the Sheriff's Department showed up after the sun disappeared below the horizon. He was a Chicano guy in his early twenties, no older than Little Joe or Jeff, and had a relaxed, polite demeanor, not at all like the cops I'd known in Chicago. He walked around the van, wondering aloud if the holes had been caused by thrown rocks instead of gunfire.

"This sort of thing happens out here, no big deal. Rowdies get out of hand and blow off a little steam. It's still the Old West, you know." He seemed intent on playing down the whole incident. After all, the van was still drivable.

The day after the attack was no time for the Seven Paths grand opening. In a somber mood, we boarded up the great holes where the windows had been. Not much serious damage besides that. We'd just begun to sweep up the glass that lay strewn all over the floor when a car pulled up. An old man, thin, with a closely trimmed moustache, hobbled out of his car, leaning on his cane. A small entourage of men in suits assisted him, informing us he was Taos Mayor Rumaldo Garcia. We set aside our brooms to greet him.

Himself a Chicano, Mayor Garcia insisted he'd come to extend his sympathy and support and wanted to see for himself what damage had been done. Using his wooden cane to knock aside some of the larger shards, he paced up and down the length of the restaurant, railing about how terrible this was for the town's economy, which was principally tourism. He and Joe sat at a table and talked. Jeff told me they'd met many times at community meetings in the past few months. The mayor's voice rose in vehemence as he declared how he meant to root out this bunch of hooligans who threatened the future of his town. That sort of behavior ruined all local businesses. We hippies were not a threat to the social order, as some claimed. We were building a respectable, if not mainstream, business. It was a boon to the local economy.

He made repeated reference to La Clinica and how it served the Chicano and Indian communities. Joe, of course, took the lion's share of credit for that as well as the community switchboard. The mayor agreed that Joe invested a lot into the community

"Look at the thanks he gets! These few violent miscreants do not represent the Mexican American culture. We needed harmony, not division, in our community."

On that note he hobbled back to his car and was driven away to check on other victims of yesterday's violence.

All those hours of artistry by Tike and Joe had been wasted. There was no immediate plan to replace the glass. On the plywood they painted anew WE ARE OPEN on one side of the door and ONLY THE GLASS WAS BROKEN on the other side in the vain hope that paying customers would flock in to let us turn a profit. Joe was worried about his cash flow. He had enough problems confronting him back in California, where his Good Karma restaurant was being stolen from him by greedy and incompetent partners. All his energy was needed here in his new enterprise.

Joe insisted that whole tribes of creative young people would be flocking to Taos that summer. We early arrivals ought to feel fortunate to have landed on his doorstep, for he was destined to be a great guru with a big following.

In India they said that when the disciple was ready, the guru would appear like magic. Maybe this Joe, a self-confessed Sage among men, would open my spiritual eyes, just as Marpa had his disciple Milarepa. The Tantric path wasn't easy. Should I stay the course and learn from him and finally make love to Tike, who could be a dakini in human form, or get the fuck out, back on my own? Weighing my options made me dizzy.

Photo Credit by John Nichols in May 1969

EXILE

"I'M PICKING UP SOME BAD goddamn vibes from one of you."
Joe stood up and, with furrowed brow, paced around the living
room, staring down into the soul of each of us. The morning had
been peaceful up to then. Joe had started out cheerful; his shipment
of pheasants was due to arrive later that day. Luckily Jeff and I had
finished fencing the bird pens, but there was still plenty to do at the
restaurant.

Here we go again. Another morning, another acrimonious breakfast meeting. Who or what had upset our Sage this time?

We'd opened the Seven Paths with the smashed-out windows
still boarded up and without the gala fanfare we'd hoped for. It would
have to do for the foreseeable future. The beautiful murals Little Joe
and Tike had slaved over were gone, like the Navajo and Tibetan sand
paintings that took days to make before they were returned as raw
materials to Mother Earth. It was a lesson in impermanence. Ready
or not, life moved on, and we had little time to dwell on misfortune.

Little Joe had reeled off his elaborate ideas for refurbishing the
restaurant. "We need to replace those windows immediately, Joe, in
defiance of the negative forces that smashed them. We'll show them
that we're not pussies!"

"Great idea," Joe's saccharine voice chided him, then his voice
hardened. "But goddamn it, man, you and Tike have wasted enough
time on those goddamn things, and we don't have the goddamn time
for that shit right now. Sure, we'll get you windows to paint, but we
have to generate some goddamned income first!"

It amazed me that Little Joe, Tike, and Jeff, who'd all come
about a month before me, put up with Joe Sage for as long as they
had. Maybe they felt that they already had too much time and energy

invested to walk away. I did too. I'd finished scouring the built-up grease off the pots and pans until they passed muster with Joe. I'd mowed the goddamn lawn that the others had let slide. Irrigating the crops that first morning, I'd endured the nonstop tongue-lashing Joe lavished on me while working at his side, despite the woozy altitude sickness I'd felt. It was all I could do to stay on my feet. I'd done my goddamnedest, never bitching, never complaining, from the moment I got there, even though I was ever more convinced that the science of macrobiotics had serious limitations. I cared about these people, our budding tribe of strangers in a strange land, and felt obligated to help them succeed.

These were my people, even *goddamn* Joe Sage, for all his faults. Old as he was, it amazed me how clueless he seemed about the most basic diplomacy needed to handle friends and influence people. No wonder he was losing his Good Karma restaurant back in California. That should have been a lesson to him. He needed each of us, not only the women, or woman, as Tike was the true Earth Woman who held all our yang hearts in her open hands. The newer girls still seemed peripheral and, enduring Joe's regular tantrums as they were, probably wouldn't stay long. I'd overheard them talking about leaving, going back to Death Valley, where, I was to learn, Charles Manson's family was based. Without Tike I'd have been long gone too. Our missed opportunity had gone on too long. That very day I was determined that even if it interrupted our work, I'd get together with her.

Our meeting droned on to other issues when Joe had suddenly stood up and began pacing around the living room with furrowed brow, as if bothered by something important. The room became silent as we waited for him to say something. Suddenly he flung out his arms, grimacing. His mood had flipped into anger, and he let us have it.

"I'm picking up some goddamn bad vibes from one of you here."

The only bad vibes I ever felt came from him. I wondered who it could be. Glancing around at the faces of our core family group— Little Joe, Jeff, and sweet, sexy Tike—they too looked bewildered, even alarmed. It was probably the two new girls that Joe had zeroed in on. They still seemed like outsiders. Leslie, despite her affectionate massage, still hadn't balled me. She always came up with some lame excuse, and as far as I knew, Joe didn't get anywhere with her either, which could be why his rage so often targeted them.

"I want some goddamn answers!" Joe raved at the top of his voice. "Whoever it is, you know who you are, and I want you to speak up!"

I was sick of the damn angry drama. Maybe it was time for me to speak up. We'd been skirting the real issue, putting off the most burning problem confronting us: bad vibes from Joe. But since he'd brought it up, we may as well clear the air so we could move on to more positive communication. At seventeen I was the youngest adult member our family. I wasn't sure how to present my high-flown ideas, but I sucked in a deep breath and forged ahead.

"I think," I began and hesitated when everyone's eyes turned to me. I was unused to speaking up in front of a crowd. Gulping, I continued, "I'm starting to think of leaving."

Joe's jaw dropped and his eyes bugged out in unfeigned shock, like it did when Jeff came running in after getting shot at. It hadn't been *me* he'd been expecting to hear from.

Shit, I'd spit out my words more decisively than I intended, but it was only an opening to the discussion. The others should jump right in. I expected to hear their thoughts, their convincing arguments that I should stay. We'd become close and shared some crazy times in the past month. Of course, we'd work it out; none of them wanted to lose me. Our grueling projects, men's work, depended on me as much as Little Joe and Jeff. The women seemed happy with lighter duties and showed no desire for the hard, manual labor required of us guys.

It took a moment for Joe to react. When he did, he exploded with greater force than I expected.

"You goddamned snot-nosed crybaby!"

Snot-nosed crybaby? I'd hoped for dialogue, not condemnation. This had gone wrong. Joe's words cut into me and threw off my momentum. I didn't know how to respond. Unless someone stepped in, echoing my thoughts, I'd be made the scapegoat. Tike slumped between Little Joe and Jeff on the opposite couch. She stared at the floor, not at me, as if wishing to be somewhere far away. They'd all been shocked speechless, even Little Joe, who could be expected to jump in at a time like this, but he looked like a deflated balloon. I couldn't tell what any of them were thinking but hoped someone would back me up.

Joe stormed around the room, yelling, repeating over and over that I was a goddamn *snot-nosed crybaby*. His intensity cut deep. I struggled to find words to get the others on board. We needed to discuss these things like *goddamn* sane adults, but all my words caught in my throat, even if Joe gave me a moment to say them. My brain froze. I couldn't articulate my jumbled feelings even to myself. My main concern was Tike.

Did Tike think I wanted to abandon her? If only I'd had a chance to speak to her. My thoughts of leaving had nothing to do with her. The memory of her warm embrace remained with me as the only convincing argument for my staying. Well, that and my rapport with Jeff, and the promise of participating in a peyote ceremony with the Taos Indians, and the dimmer promise of learning astral projection from Joe. No, I wasn't ready to leave the family yet.

Joe kept on the attack. Then he reared up to spit out his punchline.

"Your karma will follow you!"

Of course, my karma would follow me, that's what karma did. What did he mean? My conscience was clear. Or had I missed something? What if Joe was the guru my karma had destined me to train under? Guru Marpa, in ancient Tibet, had tormented the Jetsun Milarepa like a slave with abusive tasks until he had pack sores on his back. Only after he'd brought Milarepa to the tearful edge of total emotional and psychological collapse did Marpa manifest as the Tantric master who'd cleansed his karma and set him up for Buddhahood. The Tantric path was not for the fainthearted.

Would I be losing my chance, like I had as a child, turning my face from the being levitating me into some exalted experience? Maybe Joe *was* that same being. I hadn't focused enough on the face, but the eyes. Yes, Joe had piercing eyes too, maybe, but it was so long ago. Or was he a charlatan, manipulating me, using psychology to sway his power over me, over us, making each of us feel less adequate and more dependent on him? Confused, I felt like I stood between two goalposts, unsure which way to run.

"Your karma will follow you!" Joe shouted even louder, repeating it three more times, blasting his words as if pronouncing a curse. He put so much hatred into it that I couldn't help shuddering.

I'd been struggling to keep myself under control, but unable to put my words into a coherent reply, humiliated and confused, my frustration vented in unmanly tears of frustration. Unable to stop the force of nature, I felt them stream down my cheeks, shaming me, reminding me that I was a fucking loser. They were tears of never being able to do any goddamn thing right no matter how hard I tried.

"See," Joe shouted in triumph. "You're a goddamned snot-nosed brat, a little crybaby!"

Why should we men be so ashamed of our emotions and our tears? I'd read that even bold Indian warriors cried, open and unashamed at times, but I stood on unstable ground. What if the others saw my tears as signs of my guilt, my shame at the cosmic truth Joe was shouting at me? Joe was doing his best to expose me as the snot-nosed miscreant wrecker of our communal harmony. It all depended on how the others reacted. If they voiced their own concerns, we could take control of our destiny and make this so-called love commune a fit place to live.

Before anyone had a chance to say anything, Joe roared at them, "Leave him alone, goddamn it. He wants to go, let him *fucking* go! We don't need him." Then our Sage turned his back on me and, with quieter words, steered the meeting onto the pressing priorities of the current day, as if I'd already become irrelevant.

"Someone needs to stay to receive the pheasants. Leslie, you stay. The rest of us will go to the restaurant."

I didn't want to leave so abruptly, not without talking it over with each of them, but what else could I do after that deluge of abuse with no one speaking in my defense? Joe had left me no dignified way out. So I went into the bedroom closet to get my stuff, but unlike when Joanne went in to pack, no one came in to talk with me. If Tike or Jeff had spoken to me, it could have helped me rework my situation.

My money was still crumpled up in my blanket-wrapped gear, along with my remaining hoard of Space Sticks and jerky. It was a good thing I'd never mentioned the non-macrobiotic food—it would have been tossed out—or the money, which might have been offered up to community property, meaning Joe. A few days before, I'd heard Joe pressuring Jeff and Little Joe to cough up their extra assets into the common kitty. Since I'd stumbled in there with nothing more than blankets tied into a bundle, Joe didn't imagine I had any resources.

While I packed, the low drone of conversation continued in the living room as they restructured the day's tasks for fewer remaining workers. They needed me, I had no doubt about that, which proved how ridiculous it was for Joe to run me out without more of a hearing. Working as hard as the others every day that I'd been there, I deserved that much and more.

This family was no democracy. My dear companions had all been cowed into passive submission. What kind of counterculture was this anyway? I may as well stay under my workaholic dad's roof or go into the fucking Army and have a drill sergeant ride my ass if this was the only alternative culture we could come up with.

I grabbed my pathetic pile of possessions and walked back into the living room before the meeting had finished. There I stood facing them for a mute, yet still hopeful, moment. Despite all the effort I'd put in, the friendships I thought I'd formed, no farewells came my way from any of them. Joe didn't even look at me but continued droning on about his expected shipment of goddamn pheasants. Feeling like a stranger in a strange land rather than a valued member of our little community, I passed on through the living room and out the front door without a word spoken to me from anyone. Even so, I felt lighter, as if a great weight was off my shoulders as I opened the wooden gate and walked through to a new destiny.

Plenty of options lay before me. Hitchhiking, I'd go wherever my rides took me. Maybe I'd wind up at another Taos commune, one with less hollering, or find some old woman who needed a herder for her goats like the Apache Tear guys. Herding seemed the ideal career for me; I'd have time to meditate.

Sad to be leaving and yet elated to be getting away from Joe, I crossed the little bridge over the irrigation channel, my Rubicon, to confront my future. The van, with Jeff at the wheel, sped past me without stopping. Inside I saw the grim, unsmiling faces of Little Joe and Tike. I'd raised my hand to wave but too late, they were gone. Would they miss me as much as I'd miss them, or had Joe succeeded in turning them against me? Almost to the highway, another car came up from behind and pulled over with the window open. To my surprise it was Joe, and he seemed calm. He waited for me get in. I hesitated.

"You want a ride or not?"

Still smarting at his insults, I slid into the front seat beside him without a reply. He drove on without a word, which surprised me, leaving me to wonder whether he regretted exiling me from our would-be happy home, a home I'd worked my ass off for. Maybe he was waiting for me to grovel and beg to be allowed to stay, but that wouldn't be enough. Backing down from the position he put me in would mean he'd won again, as he always did, and nothing would change. A simple apology, spoken like one human being to another, would work for me.

Did I have to lay that out for him? Things couldn't go on as before. Eventually the others would give up and leave too; that seemed inevitable. All our communal effort would be wasted. Joe alone reaped the reward if he drove us all out, but he couldn't keep up with all his projects without our help.

Still, I had questions that arose from my spiritual journey. Would Joe now reveal himself as my Tantric master, like Marpa had to Milarepa? Although I didn't have pack sores on my back, it was a similar situation. Milarepa, broke and weeping, at the edge of his sanity, was on his way out the door to an uncertain future. Marpa seemed unmoved, letting him go, but Marpa's wife, a celestial dakini in human form, intervened. Only then did Marpa transform into his loving aspect, embracing Milarepa as his principal disciple on the Vajrayana, diamond path to Buddhahood. If this Sage was such a capable spiritual guide, I would stay and endure what I must, but Tike did not intervene on my behalf, and he made no sign of what Marpa had done.

Joe pulled over on the south edge of Taos, saying I'd have better luck hitching outside of town. "Good luck," he wished me as he drove away, maybe still hoping I'd come running back to him. Maybe I should have, but with a feeling of washed-out calm, like after the passing of a thunderstorm, I was elated to be free. Freedom can be bittersweet. I was on the road again but alone, already missing dear friends who'd become sudden strangers.

THE BLOOD OF CHRIST

MY FIRST RIDE CAME WITHIN minutes. The thirtyish man in shaded glasses and ponytail called out to me.

"I'm not stopping in town, mate, going straight through!"

"Me too, man! I'm done with Taos." That had been a split-second decision, and I ran with it, unimpressed with what I'd seen of hippies around there. Somewhere beyond Taos I'd find a better experiment in communal living.

"This is the best country in the world!" he shouted with unfeigned enthusiasm.

"Do you mean the USA or these New Mexico mountains?"

"Both! Let me tell ya, mate, Australia's got nothing on the States, I'm glad to be out of there. Here in the USA you have varieties of food—Mexican, Chinese, Italian, all kinds of restaurants offering international cuisine—whereas Aussie food is always the same old thing."

"I bet a Mexican restaurant would do well there."

"You'd think so, but I doubt it. The damned fools don't have enough imagination to appreciate it."

We took a left at the Y, and I craned my neck for a glance at the boarded-up windows of the Seven Paths restaurant. Jeff's van was parked outside. I pointed the place out to the Aussie as we flashed past.

"Ever tried that kind of food?" I asked.

"No, because I heard how bad their food was. No flavor whatsoever, mate. Variety of texture and taste are the spice of life, far as I'm concerned."

I could only agree with him. All that macrobiotic stuff was behind me now.

"Where are you bound, mate?"

"I've set my compass for wilder new directions. Maybe I'll explore these mountains."

"The mountains? Why, you're already up in them!" he exclaimed, as if the two-lane road we drove on was right up in the magical peaks around us.

I explained that I wanted to go deep into the wilderness on a spirit quest.

"Oh, yes, the aborigines back home, blackfellows we call them, do that sort of thing. They call it a walkabout. There is a place off the highway somewhere up ahead. Some hippies there are building a sort of American ashram. It's called Lama something or other."

That must be the place I'd heard Easy talking about in Santa Fe, where they'd hung old bomb casings up to use for gongs. The Aussie told me more about Lama, which he'd visited with some friends once. Eager to see it myself, I asked the way.

"It's up this way, somewhere off to the right." He flung his hand forward in a vague motion. "But the road isn't marked, and I can't remember which turnoff it is. You won't be able to find it on your own."

That was disappointing.

"By the way," the Aussie continued, "*Lama* means mud in Spanish. A little Mexican hamlet nearby had taken that name, which the hippies found providential as a Lama is what you call a Tibetan monk. They're trying to make their Lama an inter-faith monastery where all religions are one. I think that's a commendable idea, even if I'm not all that keen on religion myself."

The Australian dropped me off beyond Questa and sped off, leaving me alone once again in the midst of spectacular scenery. If I couldn't find Lama, I decided that I'd make my way up to my original destination: Drop City, Colorado.

Only a few minutes elapsed before another car pulled over. A man and woman dressed in flowing, colorful, tie-dyed fabric beckoned me aboard their car, which appeared overstuffed with luggage.

"You'll have to squeeze in the front seat with us," the woman called out. "The back is full." She was American and bragged that

145

the driver, her lover, who had a red bandanna wound as a turban around his head, was a real Spaniard from Spain and a student of the Southwest's colonial history.

"Where're you going?" the woman asked me.

"Drop City, near Trinidad, Colorado."

"You are on the wrong side of the mountains, my friend," the Spaniard said. "No roads go across. You've got to go way up and around, through Fort Garland and Walsenburg, but you'll enjoy these fantastic Sangre de Cristo Mountains."

The Spaniard spoke in awe of the mountains, whose white peaks, blinding bright in the sunshine, loomed to our right. He explained that *sangre* means blood in Spanish, so it's the *Blood of Christ* mountains in English.

"Can I cross them on foot?"

He laughed. "You'd need mountain gear for that, *amigo*."

We carried on an animated conversation. He'd delved deep into the historical background of the area and become quite knowledgeable about intriguing details, like the Spanish Catholic Penitential sects. Through whippings and self-torture, they abnegated the body in imitation of Christ to produce an almost masochistic ecstasy of spiritual purity.

"That was a big deal around New Mexico in the colonial times," he informed me.

I added what I knew of similar Hindu and Buddhist penances or purification practices to purge evil karma. We agreed that they had much in common with the Roman Catholic variety.

Crossing the state line into Colorado, he told me that they were only going to a farm near San Luis, a little village of a few hundred souls, only seventeen miles into Colorado.

"San Luis is the oldest town in what's now Colorado," he said. "It used to be part of New Mexico and was settled by Spanish people. We're staying with friends there." He pushed a button on the dash. "Hey, man, you gotta hear this."

The eight-track tape player began cranking out music that I hadn't heard before. The woman closed her eyes and moved with it; her flowing dance inspired me to do the same. Eyes closed to the bright sunshine, I felt myself floating with the tune without a care in the world. A movie jump-started in my mind, perhaps inspired by the song.

If I ventured in the slipstream between the viaducts of your dream…
Would you kiss-a my eyes? To lay me down. In silence easy.

Like magic Tike appeared in a flashback to our aborted tryst in the kitchen. Her smell of patchouli oil and coconut came back to me. She put one arm around my neck, like a creeping vine, pulling my face-down to her tasty, wet lips, and yes, she began kissing my eyes as I surrendered to her. Her other hand dug into my jeans to find my cock, which, both in my happy delirium and in my present reality, sprang up hard and ready for her. But even with my eyes shut, I knew it was but an unfulfilled fantasy. The dreamy music and lyrics had grabbed me back to revisit what I'd already realized was the worst sin of omission in my short life. My future would contain a great many mistakes but the most regretted always involved women.

The lyrics continued talking to me as the mental scene changed. In Tike's arms I felt her lower me into a box. A coffin? Her teary eyes looked down at me as darkness, tinged with sorrow, overwhelmed me. A chapter in my life had closed with the finality of death, and I could only mourn the loss of loved ones until destiny threw us together again. The song crooned on like a soothing mantra to wash away my anguish, reminding me that we were each a part of the vast cosmic eternity in which sorrow and fear could not last.

To be born again. To be born again…
In another time… Ain't nothing but a stranger in this world…

Death would come, as it must, but Tike and I would reassert ourselves one day to burst out of another womb, renewed, as we had for millennia.

As the music faded, I opened my eyes and turned to my companions.

"Wow, who was that? His song gave me some kind of a contact high."

The woman chuckled. "You dig it too? That's Van Morrison singing 'Astral Weeks.' We love him too, don't we, *querida*?" She nudged her man.

147

He took his eyes off the highway, smiled, and smacked his lips at her by way of an air kiss. "*Sí, mi amor.* He's like The Van, man! El Morrison is spooky-cool."

"You know it, baby," his lady said as she leaned over to plant a real kiss on his mouth that twisted her way to receive it.

A little beyond San Luis, they pulled off on a local road, bound west toward Estella. With a wave they vanished into the dusty, arid expanse. It was as if they'd never existed. I carried on north, missing their pleasant companionship, meditating on the ephemeral nature of all things.

My good luck at getting rides vanished in the hitchhiker's hell of Colorado. No one stopped and traffic was light. I remembered what the state trooper had told me about soliciting rides in that state. I'd have to be careful thumbing cars. Deciding that I may as well keep walking as wait for hell to freeze over, I shouldered my load and trudged along the shimmering ribbon of road, getting hotter in the afternoon sun. In the shattering silence of passing time, only three cars going my way flashed by. My chances of a ride didn't look promising.

I could hear the whooshing sound of a car coming from a long way back, giving me plenty of time to turn and face it without raising my thumb before I saw whether it was a cop. As another car approached, I turned to look. Shit, a cop! I swung back around and continued walking, my hands at my sides, not soliciting a ride, but I heard him pull over behind me. Not again!

The cops in this state must have better things to do than bother a guy on a stroll. Maybe he just wanted to see how I'm doing. Grim-faced and humorless behind his sunshades, he crunched across the gravel toward me.

"Where are you going?"

"Trinidad."

"You're on the wrong side of the mountains."

"I know, I gotta go around."

He gave me the same rap I'd heard before, no solicitation of a ride, but with another cruel twist. "You'll have to move onto the left side of the road, facing the approaching traffic."

That son of a bitch! I was forced to comply, crossing over under his watchful eye. He was taking away every chance of my getting a ride, maybe leaving me to die out there before the rare good-natured driver would ever spot me.

As the cop faded into the distance, I continued trudging on the wrong side of the road to be sure he didn't double back on me. Nothing would surprise me about those refined thugs. They'd do anything to make a guy's life miserable.

HEAVEN IN HELL

THE PEAKS OF THE SANGRE de Christo gleamed ice-cream white over the brown, scrub-covered earth between us. The ground seemed to stretch out flat to their base. How many miles could it be to the highway on the other side? Distances out there could be deceiving, but life needed to be lived with boldness. If I was to die, it may as well be in the mountains of Christ's Blood, seeking my guardian spirits. I'd almost no other choice. I'd seek glory with the motto *March or die.*

I thought it must be at least ten miles across in a direct line and many more going up and down the uneven terrain. In a futile gesture I re-crossed the highway to thumb one last car on the barren highway. Then I faced the distant peaks to my east, jumped over a broken-down barbed-wire fence, and kept going.

To conserve water, I stopped drinking from my canteen, which was still almost full, and placed a pebble beneath my tongue. The Apache Indians did that to keep the saliva flowing and lessen their craving for unavailable water. I wouldn't allow myself to think about thirst or panic would take over, stealing my courage and will to do what I must. I'd swallow all my spit, conserving every drop of moisture. I was sweating but biology can't be stopped. We're not lizards that are better equipped for survival in the desert, but I hoped to reach the snow line or a stream before I dehydrated and became food for buzzards and coyotes.

The dense brush clawed at me, but it didn't rip my jeans to shreds as that gay driver near Denver insisted it would. After an hour or two of hard slogging, I'd climbed up and over one, two, then three or more steep arroyos that blocked my way. When I looked back from a rise, it seemed that I was an equal distance between the road and the alluring snow peaks. They seemed within reach; maybe I'd make it by morning.

Another hour of exertion and the view looked the same, the road no farther behind me and the mountains no closer than the last time I'd looked. I could still see the glint of sunlight reflected on the windshield of a passing car on the road, but I had to be getting somewhere.

The grade began getting steeper, my breathing more difficult, and my legs ached and cramped from exhaustion as I faced what I expected to be the last foothill before the great snowcaps. I told myself I was almost there and celebrated with another rare swig from my canteen. I'd have to stop a few more times, but not too long because I'd be there soon. I'd rest then with snow's runoff to quench my thirst.

Following faint animal trails where I could made the going easier, but they zigzagged up and down too much. I abandoned them for a more direct route, ever upward.

The dying sun turned the brushy landscape a royal color, deep purple, as I bivouacked for the night. I'd had nothing to eat since the sugarless oatmeal at that morning's disastrous breakfast. No longer a macrobiotic, I enjoyed the life-affirming taste and nutrition of my remaining Space Sticks. Peanut butter clung to the back of my throat. To wash it down I permitted myself a last swallow from my canteen. About a fourth of it remained for tomorrow morning's trek. I guesstimated that I'd be at the snow line by afternoon at the latest. Not bothering with a fire, I curled up under the shelter of a bush, wrapped in the cocoon of my two Army blankets.

The night passed restfully. On occasion I woke to listen to the animals, night stalkers hunting in the vicinity. Owls hooted and what may have been a coyote's brief, yapping howl soothed my soul. The only sound I dreaded was the slithering of a rattlesnake into my blankets, but the night was too cold for them.

In dreamland I frolicked with Tike, my vivacious blond Earth Mother. Oh, Tike! But awaking, I knew my dreams scolded me, reminding me that I'd been a fool to let Joe's head games block me from making sweet love to her. If I'd consummated our mutual desire, things should have turned out better for both of us. We'd have bonded tighter, become less susceptible to Joe's raging turmoil. She wouldn't have sat staring at the floor while Joe lambasted me. No, she'd have risen to my defense, as if she gave a fuck about me.

Standing together, we'd force Joe to back off, calm down, become a goddamn human being. Sure, he could drive me away, but he would never bear to lose Tike with no other desirable woman in sight. Sound Current Ranch could then remain our home with good vibes and general affection for old and young alike. We'd make more babies, share the parenting and partnering, and become an inspiration to aspiring communes throughout the nation.

Damn, I'd blown it by leaving. Joe's curse still reverberated in my mind: *Your karma will follow you.* Maybe I was a goddamn snot-nosed baby, like he'd said. Reliving that scene in my mind almost convinced me to return and hash it out with him. Joe fostered my sense of inadequacy. I'd had to escape him, but in doing so I also lost Tike. I'd abandoned her.

It wasn't only me. We'd let Joe divide and control us. We had strength in numbers if we'd held to our fraternal bond and stuck up for each other. We were free labor for Joe Sage to enrich himself at our expense. How long could it take before the others left too, their pockets empty, their labor wasted?

Why did he have to ride us so hard? Joe's unnecessarily harsh behavior seemed counterproductive as we were a willing workforce. That saddened as much as it rankled me because I wanted the concept of a communal tribe to succeed.

Buddha taught interdependence. Without exception every one of us has a mother and wants a lover. We are all interconnected, as friends, enemies, parents, and so on, and those roles changed, enemies into friends or lovers, if all went well. Without Joe I would not have met Tike, without the fortuitous ride with the ranter I'd not have met Joe, and Easy Rider dropped me where he'd find me. Our relationships became complicated by our confusion. Greed and aversion, that's our Samsara.

Our very existence depends on others, as does our salvation from the insanity of Samsara. In the Mahayana great vehicle, liberation is a team effort. Thinking about the great vow of the Bodhisattva—to return again and again into the burning house of Samsara to save all—brought tears to my eyes. No one can be left behind, condemned to hell as in certain faiths. Our own salvation, our true happiness becomes hollow, incomplete, without each of them.

Shivering in the dewy, predawn light before the full power of the sun was upon me, I roused myself to march. Damn it, I felt great! I'd always been a morning person. Even if I died out there, it would be a clean death, glorious somehow. I was in the middle of a desert and tried to put thoughts of Tike and Joe behind me. Finding water came first! Even so, I couldn't stop thinking about them.

I topped another rise before the full light of day and could no longer see the long, thin ribbon of road behind me. That meant I was higher in the mountains, closer to water. Like the day before, I had no established trail to guide me and encountered long ridges. After I climbed them, I found that they snaked off to the north or to the south, leaving me with the choice of following the changing course along the ridge or descending back into the valley and up on the other side, only to find another ridge beyond. All I could do was pray for the guidance of Manitou, Wakan Tanka, Usen, Christ, or Buddha, whichever name we apply to powerful entities who were there to guide us.

At the top of yet another ridgeline, the dry brush finally gave way to forested alpine country. Among pine trees I walked along the meandering ridge to avoid retaking the heights I'd exhausted myself to win, but to my disappointment I found that ridge, too, curved back around.

My canteen was almost empty. I was getting desperate, which gave me a demonic energy. Back down I went, running and leaping, almost flying, then trudging with fierce resolve up another steep and grueling climb to the other side, where I found myself confronted with yet another meandering ridge. Sisyphus must feel like this, I imagined as I sucked air and rested my limbs again. Little by little I was gaining altitude, but it took a lot out of me.

My surroundings became ever greener; I came across the rutted trails of elk and their human hunters. The human sign appeared old.

They'd been cruising in jeeps that left deep scars on the trail. The hunters had abandoned cans and bottles and occasionally hung up the rotting carcass of a sheep on a stretch of barbed-wire fence along the trail. Had they done it for target practice, or were these carcasses poisoned to kill coyotes?

A few drops of amber liquid lay in an abandoned bottle along the trail, the label too faded to read. Tempted, I tried it. *Yech*! I spit out the vinegary taste and consumed the very last drops in my canteen to clear my throat and control my nausea. I struggled to keep from retching out even more of my precious body fluid. I had to find water, or I'd die out there. I finished the last of my Space Sticks and licorice squares. I felt a little guilty about that. Ordinarily I should have been fasting if I was trying to commune with the supernatural, but since I was exerting myself in crossing mountains rather than waiting quietly for a vision, I needed to eat, and it was little enough. The spirits would forgive my gluttony. They were testing me, I had to bear up!

Another day was done. The sweet smell of conifer and sagebrush did nothing to allay my thirst and rising panic as I tried to sleep. Would I make it? It had been folly to go wandering into these mountains without enough food or water or even a proper sleeping bag. Would I die, unmourned, my corpse devoured to whitened bone fragments that would blend in, unnoticed, with these elk and sheep skeletons all around me? Who would think anything about it even if they stumbled upon some articulated bones way out there?

That struck me as funny; I laughed out loud at the thought of my death. Why not? From somewhere deep inside of me an irrepressible mirth sprang up. Maybe it was the thin oxygen because I must have been at about nine or ten thousand feet.

The next morning, I sprang up with insane confidence. I'm not dead yet, hell no! I had to keep on anyway, so why not be happy until the end? This Sangre de Cristo had been *my* choice, I couldn't blame another. Come what may, it was my responsibility to make it. If the spirits wouldn't give me their tangible support, it's their loss, fuck 'em! That thought cracked me up. Maybe I was crazy and about to perish, but I was having a great time. Then I saw it.

Covered with fallen pine needles, it was a small, brown hump the size of a sleeping man or a grave. That looked odd; it didn't belong there under the trees. I scraped off a layer of pine needles to find hard, crusted snow, all that was left of winter's snowfall. I'd been saved!

I broke off a small snowball to suck on. It was good but colder than I needed, weak and shivering as I was. The snow melted in my mouth to an inconsequential trickle. I craved a mouthful, a big gulp of wet, delicious water, but that was not to be had so easily. It was agonizing to wait while I packed as much as I could into my canteen, hoping it would soon melt into that intoxicating, most satisfying of beverages: water.

Moving on, I found more mounds of debris-covered snow. I was getting closer to the snow line. Finally, I heard a low roaring up ahead. After rounding another corner, I saw it at last: a waterfall cascading down a steep, moss-covered slide of rocks. Bursting with joy, I ran up and leapt under it, drinking my fill of sacred, life-giving water.

It was freezing yet refreshing after my sweaty exertions. I stripped off my clothes and, whooping and hallooing, washed in the frigid waters, showering off the dust and grime of the past two days' hard traveling. Then, after rinsing my clothes and laying them out, I sat naked in the hot sun to dry and warm my bones. Shivering, I should have been exhausted but felt refreshed and giddy.

This was a sacred spot as far as I was concerned. So with the melodic rush of the water beside me, I attempted to meditate but found it impossible to concentrate on anything but my immediate problems. I had water but no food and knew the giddiness was from my exertion in the high, thin air. I had to move on and obtain more of the necessities of life, but first I offered prayers to the spirits who'd led me there, all the while knowing that it was much more my own efforts as the aid of the unseen.

Out there in the mountains sacred to the blood of Jesus, I had time to sort out and accept some realities. Harsh speech was the secret of Joe's power. Cussing helped to focus his energy like a black-magic mantra. If I was to survive in a world that *does not* belong to the meek, I'd need to handle that kind of energy myself. I'd have to wash out the guilt trip Joe laid on me and shout back in the face of madness to channel my own visceral power.

Snot-nosed baby indeed. Fuck him! The distance I'd put between us hadn't silenced Joe's cutting words nor even my father's more distant voice. Their words continued ringing in my ears; it was no use pretending they didn't. Words cut deep into the soul of a feeling person. I needed to confront the power of words to process the deeper psychic wounds and rechannel my unvoiced rage at the injustice. To let it ride, remain self-effacing without countering evil, was not, in my analysis, a virtue. My silent acquiescence had left me not sainted but crippled, unable to be assertive and do what needed doing in a world that granted little time to respond and stopped for no one. No longer should I hold my tongue when confronted with bastards like Joe.

Joe could have been a mentor, a friend, but chose to be an angry tyrant. Although he'd never laid a hand on me, he harmed me, harmed us all, but most of all he harmed himself. Thoughts were more powerful than yin-yang balanced food. It wasn't brown rice alone that would change our world. We had to stop the bullshit and reach out to each other. This was hardly a novel idea—it was as old as Buddha's message—but we had to reaffirm this truth again and again to make it happen in our present.

I pondered all this while drinking again and again from the sweet nectar flowing down the mossy, green rocks from on high. This high point in my life had made all my perambulations to get there worthwhile. I was at the mountaintop, there was no one riding my ass, I was as free as anyone, but where would I go from there? Eventually I'd have to eat. The spirits, or my own conscience, had shown me all they were willing to at the time, and I'd better drop back down to civilization.

Climbing above the waterfall I'd encounter steep ridges, no telling how many, until I reached the road on the far side. This range of mountains was over thirteen thousand feet elevation. It looked too taxing a feat in my worn-out condition without any food. Following the little creek issuing from the waterfall seemed the best idea. It angled north in the direction of Fort Garland, where I could bus around the mountains if I didn't get a ride. I'd all but given up on hitchhiking in Colorado. It was nineteen miles from San Louis to Garland if I'd kept to the road. The trip into the mountains had added many more miles, but the sheer adventure had been worth it.

Ojito Creek was the name of the stream, I later saw on a map of the region. Coming down along its banks was much easier than climbing up. Soon I was out of the trees and back in flat chaparral country with extensive Jeep trails. Then there were corrals and pools dug out for cattle to drink, although no animals were present, and I didn't encounter any people either. Finally, the stream turned south, although I could see the long ribbon of the highway straight ahead. I left the water and jogged due west to meet Route 159.

As soon as I got there, with amazing serendipity, a Greyhound bus hove into view. Jumping up and down, I waved. The great silver beast lumbered to a halt and I climbed aboard.

"I'm just taking this bus into Fort Garland," the smiling driver informed me. "You can get another one there if you're going any farther." He waved me aboard, refusing to charge me as we were so close to town. His kind attitude improved my image of the people of Colorado.

The seats were empty except for a cowboy kissing and fondling his girlfriend in the middle of the bus and an old man sleeping in the back. It was getting dark. Fort Garland held historical attractions from the era of Kit Carson, but I was starving and too tired to check them out. I ate the special in the diner, finishing in time to race aboard my next bus. Paying the fare demanded with my dwindling cash, I took the seat right behind the driver, who spoke to me of legends of the Old West.

On winding roads, we climbed northeast into the mountains, crossing North La Veta Pass at 9,413 feet, encountering snow flurries that made me shiver and pull my blankets close around me. The bus climbed down into Walsenburg, where I disembarked to board another bus for the ride south to what had been my initial destination weeks ago. It had been a long digression. Trinidad, Colorado at last! This long journey through the night was over. It was early morning, but I'd slept as much as I could on the way and was ready for another adventure.

DROP CITY

LEAVING THE BUS STATION IN Trinidad, I asked directions and was pointed up the road toward El Moro, eight miles away. That was the tiny hamlet to the north near where the hippie enclave of Drop City was located. After a short walk, a car pulled over. In the front seat was a couple who appeared to be about forty. The woman spoke up.

"Are you by any chance going to Drop City?"

I hesitated, taken by surprise. "Why, yes, I am." I jumped in the back seat next to a young man with short, black hair who I assumed was their son. He sat staring ahead, as impassive and wordless as a statue.

"Do you happen to know the way?" the man driving asked.

"Should be straight ahead. Watch for domes or anything colorful on the landscape."

They'd driven down for the day from Pueblo, eighty-five miles to the north. The man wore a colorful Hawaiian, short-sleeved shirt that inadequately covered his massive belly, upon which a camera nestled. He looked so much like a typical suburbanite on vacation that I almost laughed. While they dressed like my parents, they manifested a keen, open-minded interest in the hippie phenomenon and communal life. Perhaps not so different from me, they too were searching for a little more meaning in their lives.

The directions were adequate, and we soon saw a collection of colorful geodesic domes arise from the scrubland and parked in a graveled parking lot off the road. The guy who sat beside me grabbed his backpack and got out. I realized then that he'd been a hitchhiker like me, another youthful pilgrim rather than the couple's son. His close-cut, black hair indicated a school's dress code that he'd recently escaped. He wore sandals and a brown, Mexican serape or poncho over what looked like dirty white pajamas, such as Mexican peasants wore in Western movies. I tried but failed to engage him in conversation. He spoke only when spoken to and answered with as few words as possible. His eyes looked like he may have been stoned or coming down from such a heavy trip that words seemed redundant.

Immediately a young brunette lady in glasses came out to meet us, greeting us in a cordial fashion and asking us two hitchhikers if we intended staying the night. This question must have flustered my new *amigo*; he mumbled something that sounded noncommittal, but I told her straight out that I'd be grateful to accept their hospitality. The lady was garbed in a ballooning, psychedelic hippie dress that was begrimed and toil-worn yet still colorful. She smelled of spices and homey wood smoke, nineteenth-century kitchen scents. Acting the gracious hostess, she offered to show us around.

The first stop was the community center in front of which we stood. It consisted of three geo-domes that had been joined together, like the symbol of the trinity. As the name implied, this large space was for eating and large gatherings. There was a spacious, if grubby, kitchen in which a few others, mostly women, went about their business without paying any mind to us strangers. Across the way a little, wooden stairway led up to something like an Oriental pasha's lounging room, replete with India prints and pillows scattered around the floor and several low couches.

Outside were clotheslines upon which hung a colorful assortment of clothes and bedding. If the residents were not spotlessly clean, it was not for want of the effort put out by the Droppers. They had plumbing and running water in the community dome, but there is only so much you can do in a virtual desert with rudimentary resources. This was still a pioneer settlement, and the poverty and lack of twentieth-century amenities gave the place an atmosphere like a psychedelic *Tobacco Road*. However, these Droppers were, as a rule, a better-educated set of hillbillies with an artistic bent.

As I soon learned, most of the founding members, like the celebrated Peter Rabbit, had moved some distance away and founded another commune named Libra. Others were away in distant cities, attending to a variety of creative projects, not least of which was earning money, that despised but so necessary thing hippies called *bread*. There was poverty, although accepted for the most part by these Droppers with good cheer. In modern America money talked; without it life crawled along with fewer options.

The tour over, the generous tourists from Pueblo offered to lay some bread, several greenbacks, on the grateful Dropper chick. She'd made a low-key pitch for donations during her tour of the domes and thanked them profusely, so I knew her for a realist and admired her for it. Even so, I felt a twinge of embarrassment at the necessity. They had to perform like colorful natives for the patronizing tourist. Tourists, I'd remembered reading in the Time-Life *Hippie* book, were one of the principal incomes for this commune. It wasn't financially self-sufficient.

These rather wistful benefactors seemed reluctant to leave. Perhaps they were fishing for an invitation to stay and join the Dropper commune? None had been offered them, perhaps due to the perceived age gap with those presently in residence. We two youthful pilgrims, however, were told by this pleasant Dropper hostess to make ourselves at home and find something to eat in the kitchen if we were hungry. The short-haired guy mumbled something about not being sure if he wanted to stay and went outside to sit by the front entrance to the community dome, where he remained while I took her up on the offer. I was hungry and thrilled to hear any sort of welcoming sound, believing this had to be the place for me to stay at last. I'd come home!

There wasn't an obsession with a strict regulated diet. A few of the women didn't eat meat, although they didn't make a big deal about it. That was a refreshing attitude after Joe's uncompromising macrobiotics. The Droppers even bragged about living off America's trash. They were people after my own heart in that regard. Recycling was a part of their mission to counter the rampant waste of resources that dominated the American lifestyle.

The best place to see this in action was the kitchen. Most of the vegetables I saw were wilted or needed rotten spots removed, having been salvaged from grocery store garbage bins. The Droppers made a practice of asking stores what surplus produce they intended throwing away. Then there were the giant sacks of dry molasses, originally meant as cattle feed. I helped unload a shipment of them from a truck to pile in a corner of the kitchen. They'd bought it dirt cheap, much cheaper than honey or sugar intended for humans.

Although it was intended for cattle, they insisted that it was good enough for humans. I tried it. It was a grainy, sticky mix of molasses and what looked like oat husks and bits of grain worked into it, but it tasted okay to me. Some of the Droppers grabbed handfuls of the stuff in passing and munched on it like candy. It was refreshing to have a few more flavors in my diet. I could sweeten my oatmeal and tea again.

"Are you staying?" asked the friendly lady of the dome.

"I'd really like to, if it's all right with everyone."

"It'll be okay. What about your friend?"

"I just met him and don't really know the guy, but I'll check on him."

"Is he okay?" she asked with concern on her face, having noticed, as I had, that he seemed under duress of some kind.

After eating I went out to sit with him along the side of the dome. Hunched over his haversack, he appeared despondent. When I walked up, he looked at me with big, doleful eyes.

"I'm leaving now," he said.

"You just got here, what's the rush?" I tried to dissuade him. After all, I'd just gotten there too and felt sympathetic. He looked at me with irritation.

"Just do your own thing, man! You got your bag and I got mine. Dig?"

It was evident he didn't want anyone crowding him. I let him be and went back inside, where I told the solicitous dome lady that he just wanted to do his own thing, whatever that was, and be left alone. Within the hour he vanished like an apparition, back on the road to everywhere and nowhere. I wondered why anyone would bother to come all the way out there if he intended to scram so fast. The guy didn't even take the time to look around or talk to anyone in the hour or two of his visit.

Used to keeping busy, I tried to contribute and be useful, but there wasn't much going on besides domestic upkeep. Drop City was almost empty of men when I came. A skeleton crew remained, mostly women with their children and a couple guys I only saw a few times because they were always out scrounging. When they delivered truckloads of produce or scrap metal, I'd help them unload it. That let me feel like I'd contributed something, but they didn't invite me, a stranger, on their resupply expeditions. There was nothing else for me to do except chip in washing dishes and sweeping the kitchen floor with the ladies of the domes.

From all the fasting I'd done in the mountains, I felt ravenous all the time. I feasted on whatever extra food they had, and there was plenty of it. Almost all the food came from America's garbage wasteland, consisting for the most part of lentil beans and rice, mixed with great quantities of overcooked green vegetables. I supposed the greens had been cooked so well because they were much closer to rotten than fresh, but I wasn't picky or a spoiled gourmand. It all tasted fine to me, washed down with a cup or two of chamomile tea. This being the first time I'd tasted that yellow tea, our standard fare, I asked the women about it.

"We pick some of it ourselves," the sociable Drop Lady boasted. "It grows wild over there."

She waved me over and I followed along to where she showed me spindling plants with bright-yellow buds that grew close to the ground. "We pick the buds and they grow back. Chamomile is good for the digestion and soothes the spirit."

The gritty sorghum grew on me too. Although I felt guilty doing so little but eating so much, no one held it against me. There was one disagreeable result of my heavy-on-cooked-greens diet: that was intestinal gas. My belly rumbled, producing farts that stank far worse than any I'd smelled before, but there wasn't anything I could do about it until I varied my diet.

The women, to my profound dismay, were all mated up with someone, whether present or out working elsewhere. Less than enthusiastic about my intrusion into their social life, they gave me looks that told me I wasn't welcome, giving me no opportunity to alter my celibate existence. Despite the wild stories I'd heard, there were no orgies, at least none that I was invited to, and I soon became bored. The dome lady told me I could explore some of the empty domes and sleep wherever I chose to.

I withdrew to the solitude of a small dome that I was told was the Drop Zone, a cozy place for retreats, with a tidy library of paperback books, including the Hindu Upanishads. I took the opportunity of perusing them until sleep overwhelmed me. With no demands placed on me, I established a pattern of napping, reading, and meditating, recovering at my leisure over several days from my grueling journey.

THROWING THE CHING

THE *I CHING BOOK OF Changes* caught my eye, the Dutton paperback edition translated by John Blofeld. A year before I'd read Carl Jung's foreword to it. Although I hadn't grasped the principles in full, Jung's recommendation gave the book credibility to me. Tike had shown me her hard copy of the *Ching*. She kept it wrapped in yellow cloth with yarrow sticks and aromatic incense, like a sacred object. She'd promised to throw the sticks and read my fortune, but busy as we were, she never got around to it. With time on my hands for once in my life, I took it up, looking for answers and direction.

It took me a whole sunny afternoon to carefully read the book's instructions, wading through the concept of the hexagrams and how to figure them until I'd grasped how to use it. The yarrow sticks were too complicated. Blofeld advised old Chinese coins as a fallback. I used three well-worn nickels instead because I was far from China. Tossing them, I came up with hexagram number seven.

Shih the Army. I wasn't sure if that boded well. Was I destined for Vietnam like most of my generation? I read on:

> Persistence in a righteous course brings to those in authority...freedom from error... Making progress with a highly dangerous task is a way of obtaining control of the realm and of winning the people's allegiance... An army is built up through discipline; without it, corruption leading to disaster occurs...

I tossed the coins again, throwing hexagram 56:

Lu the Traveler, success in small matters. Persistence with regard to traveling brings good fortune... The timely application of this hexagram is of great importance... The superior man employs wise caution in administering punishments and does not suffer the cases to be delayed.

That sounded more relevant. Was it telling me that I should hit the road again soon? I pondered over it, trying to make these ancient and obscure voices give me some deeper insight into planning my next course of action.

Reading on, I found: "Trifling with unimportant matters, the traveler draws upon himself calamity... *the calamity attendant upon having no will of our own.*"

This last part seemed to speak directly to me. I'd been under Joe's power in Taos. Leaving there *must* have been the right thing to do after all, thereby winning back my own will. I felt more justified in my sudden departure, but it still didn't stop the gnawing guilt I agonized over. I'd abandoned those I cared about. *Your karma will follow you* still rang in my head, accusing me of selfishness or a lack of love and fortitude.

What else could I have done? It was easy to imagine that I could have stood up to Joe. Maybe all of us should stand up to oppressors. The GIs in Vietnam too, goddamn it, maybe they all could stand up and refuse to obey their direct orders. But I knew in the real world, questioning and disobeying orders takes practice and experience, people skills that most of us mortals must hone over time. The money, power, and experience were all on Joe's side.

The *I Ching* helped give me some distance from my situation, a wider perspective so I could broaden the analysis of my life. Ancient words coming from a remote distance took the edge off life's never-ending drama. After two or three days of reading and meditating on my own, I felt rested up enough to plan my next venture. A lot of options were pulling me in different directions.

Should I go back to Taos, or should I stay and try to be a part of Drop City? Maybe I should forget Edgar Cayce's prophecies and move on to California, or back to Gallup and the Hopi lands. Maybe I should even go back to *sweet home Chicago* and join SDS to help bring the revolutionary counterculture to fruition there. The last choice began to make sense; we needed a real revolution in this country.

A blond guy in his early twenties returned from an extended jaunt around the country and sought out my companionship. On long talking walks we discovered we had much in common. He too was a recent émigré from suburban America looking for his tribe. We wandered far into the scrubland, scaring up lizards and gophers from the sparse vegetation. Circling back around to the domes, we walked past the only straight house in the neighborhood. The juxtaposition of this solidly middle-class frame house with a lawn of lush, green grass, the only lawn within sight of the domes, seemed surreal, as if it had been teleported from the less arid Midwest. Surrounding the rest of Drop City was only the scraggly growth of weeds and brush sprouting from barren soil. Three school-age kids were playing baseball on the lawn.

"Do you want play a game with us?"

The friendly faces of the kids dropped into disappointment when we begged off. I'm sorry to say we were too preoccupied with our wide-ranging conversation. The Droppers had long befriended these neighbors; in fact, cordial relations were the norm with the wider community. There was no hippie war there.

A fellow named Jeremy returned from the road to a hearty welcome from the Dropper community. With long, stringy, blond hair that went midway down his back, making up for the round bald spot on top, he wore a multicolored dashiki and spoke with a pronounced Cockney accent. Jeremy invited me and the blond guy to join him with a couple other guys on a drive into town.

Trinidad proved a quiet little town. The people seemed unusually friendly from long acquaintance. We ambled into a little juke joint of a café, where Jeremy and his pals speed-rapped about a million high-sounding concepts and plans for Drop City that led off in every direction. Being a stranger, I couldn't fit into the conversation. I bought a postcard and a stamp at the counter, filled it out with the usual nonsense that says nothing about what's really happening in my life, and popped it in the mail. It was my first message home since leaving.

As I followed them out of the café, a huge roll of paper money dropped from Jeremy's inadequate pocket. It was probably all the bread he had.

"Jeremy," I called, chasing after him. "You dropped this."

"What, that's mine?" He seemed embarrassed but, after checking that it was all there, turned grateful. "A lot a blokes would a peeled off a chunk a this or kept the whole bloody thing. Thanks, mate, it's a year's worth a savings, it is."

That broke the ice between us. He began including me in their conversations on the way back. A statuesque, platinum-blond woman I hadn't seen before greeted Jeremy with a warm hug and a kiss when we returned.

"This is me, old lady," he explained, and after he told her about the money, she hugged me too.

She'd arrived with him and had been resting from their journey. That afternoon, as I helped her hang laundry on the clothesline, she asked me if I was happy there and questioned me about my long-range plans. She was probably just making conversation, but I imagined that even she could see that I was muddled about which direction to take. That made me think long and hard about my situation. I needed to be more productively employed.

I'd come out west with the idea to join a commune. The West was beautiful, but in the Midwest the soil was better, and irrigation wasn't needed. My experience in Taos showed me how *not* to do it. I didn't want to usurp anyone's land, like the Chicanos in Taos feared. We had to learn from our mistakes and build warmer social connections if we were to live together in peace. Somehow, we needed to join all disenfranchised people together and create a common political front. Also, we could more directly influence mainstream culture in the cities instead of hiding out in the desert.

Jeremy had told me many of the residents of Trinidad lived below the poverty line. It was an economically depressed area. There weren't any jobs close by; that's why Dropper men went as far afield as California to scare up paying work. By that time, I was broke, with less than five dollars hiding in my watch pocket like Grandpa advised me. Why didn't I return to Chicago to find work, make some bread, and find fellow travelers interested in starting a commune back there? The sooner I got back to Chicago, the sooner I'd find a job to make enough to put my plan into action. All in good time, I decided. I'd take a few more days, get to know some of these Droppers, especially Jeremy's warm and beguiling old lady. She oozed good vibes my way. Maybe they had an open relationship.

THE ATCHISON, TOPEKA, AND SANTA FE RAILWAY

NEW GUYS SHOWED UP, COLLEGE students studying architecture. They said the domes had been inspired by Buckminster Fuller, a man they called a great visionary of the twentieth century. One, a talkative redhead, hung out, rapping with me outside the community dome. I filled him in about my time in Taos.

"Where will you go from here?" he asked.

"Well, I'm thinking of going back to Chicago. I need to make some bread, man, before I get back on the trail. Right now, I'm flat broke. I'd starve if it weren't for all the great free food around here."

"Yeah, man, Drop City is super groovy, a great place to chill out and get your head together. That's its purpose, after all. You can meet people passing through from all over the country, even the world. We can trade ideas and help each other out."

"Yeah, I'll hate to leave here. Also, I'm not looking forward to hitchhiking through Colorado. The cops don't leave you alone and threaten to throw you in jail. I've had too many run-ins with them already."

"Hey, I could help you there, man. My father is a doctor. A doctor's family members get free passes to ride the railroads. That way doctors can make house calls and travel to conferences and not be separated from their kids too long."

I'd never heard of that. The official-looking pass he showed me had no photo, just a statement that the bearer was the child of a doctor who was granted free passage on the railroad. It seemed too good to be true, and I wasn't sure if it was phony, but it couldn't hurt to try.

"Just mail it back to me when you get where you're going," he said.

"Where would I mail it?"

"Send it here, in care of Drop City, El Moro, Colorado."

In the cool night air outside the domes that evening, all of us were sitting around a campfire, roasting marshmallows, of all things, and popping corn. Jeremy's old lady heard from the doctor's son that I was leaving the next day.

She gave me a sad, disappointed look. "You're leaving already? We were just getting to know you, Ron!"

That saddened me. I stared into the fire, thinking how I would love to get to know her better too. "Well, I hadn't told him I'd set a date to leave just yet, but yeah, I gotta go make some bread. Maybe then I'll come back here and see you guys."

"We might not be here when you do," said Jeremy. "In a few months we'll be back on the road again. The bloody world's a great big place, and we want to see all of it, don't we, dear?"

She nodded agreement, if a little reluctantly. She'd been the only Dropper woman to talk to me with genuine affection. Technically she was Jeremy's old lady—that's what he called her, anyway—but she had a mind of her own and was not glued to his side, and I was still enamored with the concept of open relationships. Polygamy and polyandry, all manner of polys seemed like the best way to love, going beyond the narrow confines of monogamy.

We all needed love. If you can't make love to your friends, who can you make love to? We were becoming friends, but I didn't want to upset Jeremy and didn't have enough time to take it farther with her. Time was something I felt like I was running out of. In truth I had all the time in the world, but I felt that life was racing by, and I was missing out on something bigger, more meaningful than just hanging out, eating, and sleeping.

These Droppers were all right; they'd given me sustenance without making any demands. In Drop City I ate my fill free of charge, sunned myself, and wandered around without a work schedule or itinerary. But I felt out of place, without a girl and disconnected from any meaningful activity, like bringing the revolution into reality. The last few days had been the most relaxing I'd ever had, but if I was serious about getting a commune going or delving into radical politics, I had to be practical and make some money first.

The next morning the doctor's son took me to the train station in Trinidad. He waited while I showed my pass to the conductor. The man asked how far I was going, and I said Chicago. He nodded his head, handed me a ticket, and told me to take a seat. It worked!

I waved *adios* to my benefactor, took my seat by a window, and sat back to enjoy the ride on the Atchison, Topeka and Santa Fe Railway. Who wouldn't enjoy speeding through the beautiful countryside and for free? It was far more comfortable than hitchhiking across the miles to my destination. I almost felt guilty, like I was cheating fate to be in the lap of luxury, watching the western landscape roll by until it transformed into greener vistas before we crossed the Mississippi and I reentered Illinois.

Although I had a through ticket to Chicago, I decided going into the city and then backtracking twenty miles was too far out of my way. Joliet was the last stop before Chicago, home of the famous penitentiary. All I had to do was hitch north from there, and I'd be home in Wood Dale.

Jumping off the train in Joliet, I felt like a stranger in this no-longer familiar place. I found Highway 53, which would take me up to within a few blocks of my home in Wood Dale, but then I got a bad case of the willies, feeling apprehensive at the prospect of hitchhiking again after my experiences with Colorado cops. With my luck I might even have to walk the whole thirty-seven miles.

I decided to call my folks and tell them I was coming. Except for that postcard in Trinidad, mailed about two days ago and which probably hadn't arrived, I hadn't called or written since the day I left. It seemed so much longer than it actually was. Every day I'd been gone had been packed with so much adventure, so many amazing events.

I dropped a dime in a pay phone and called my folks. The strained voices of my mother and father on the other end didn't sound ecstatic to hear from me.

"Where are you calling from?" Mom asked.

"I'm back in Illinois, calling from Joliet."

"You're back, huh? How soon will you be here?"

"Well, I'll be hitchhiking up fifty-three." Thinking better about it, I added, "If you want, you could drive down Route 53 and meet me along the way?" It was hard to admit to Mom that I'd lost my nerve about hitching.

"No, it's late. Dad has to work in the morning. We'll just see you when you get here, goodbye."

Sticking out my thumb at passing cars, I kept walking, hopeful that someone would stop. An hour later and I still hadn't gotten a ride, but at least I'd made it beyond Joliet. As I walked my inconvenient gear kept slipping out of my blanket roll, as ever, requiring me to stop and rearrange it. That had been a problem from the beginning.

I passed a roadhouse with rowdy greasers and jocks drinking booze in the parking lot. They shouted, cursing drunkenly at me as I passed. I must have looked like a refugee in the land of my birth. I almost wished I could join them, sit down with a beer, and flirt with a cocktail waitress. But I was underage and broke.

Route 53 seemed to go on forever. Finally, I caught a ride, but it only took me a few miles up the road, where I resumed walking and vainly thumbing. Then I got a second ride that dropped me another mile or so from where he picked me up. I was getting so little mileage from so few rides that it depressed me further. It looked as rideless as Colorado except that I wasn't in the empty desert.

I contemplated camping alongside the road until morning, when my luck might be better, but decided against it. There weren't many areas away from houses where I'd be left alone. Better to keep on through the night.

Another car pulled over behind me. Turning around, I was amazed to see that it was my parents. They'd come to get me after all. I never thought I'd be so relieved to see them, but I was.

"We saw you coming down," Dad said, "but before we turned around, you'd gotten picked up. We followed until he dropped you off."

They were tired; it'd been a long night for them. I spun a condensed and censored version of my adventures, which was all they wanted to hear anyway.

It was a few more days before my postcard arrived from Colorado. By that time I'd gotten a job at Beeline Fashions in Bensenville as a stock boy. I never liked the *boy* part of that job title, but at least I was making almost a hundred dollars a week clear, more with overtime. I stayed in my old room, paying rent to my parents, which gave me a certain de facto independence. The girls I met at work were a few years older than I and had attended my high school. Other than that, we didn't have much in common. I never got anywhere with them, but I didn't try very hard either. I knew I didn't belong there.

Taking the train or biking into Chicago on my days off, I haunted head shops, bought underground newspapers like the *Chicago SEED, Kaleidoscope,* and *Rising Up Angry.* I looked around for a compatible scene to blend into, but I didn't tell anyone that my return home was only temporary. I'd stick around only long enough to save a few hundred bucks, and then I'd hit the road again.

My trip west had expanded my horizons and showed me both the positives and problems of the alternative culture scene. There were serious disappointments, like the tyranny of Joe Sage and the conflicts with the Chicanos that I attributed to a lack of tact or sensitivity, but my faith in communal life wasn't dimmed. We needed to learn how to live together, to be more inclusive, to share and bond better as equals and avoid giving too much power to one person.

Magical 1969 wasn't over; I couldn't let the revolution start without me. Later that summer I vanished into the Chicago underground. That adventure—dealing with homelessness, love on the road, SDS, the Black Panthers, and New York Motherfucker collectives—takes another book. Stay tuned, dear reader.

ABOUT THE AUTHOR

BORN IN CHICAGO, RONALD GREW up in the suburb of Wood Dale, Illinois, longing for a more meaningful life. At fifteen he ran away to New Orleans, where he lived on Skid Row until betrayed by a priest. As a disaffected seventeen-year-old high school dropout in 1969, Ronald took LSD while hitchhiking into the western American counterculture world of not so free-love communes. He also became involved in radical movements in New York and Chicago, including the SDS Days of Rage. He was arrested and subjected to several months in a mental hospital before returning to participate in the counterculture, joining a Wisconsin commune, which remained his home throughout the 1970s.

In 1975 he hitchhiked across North Africa and the Middle East, spent time on a kibbutz and working at a copper mine in Israel's Negev desert. Then on to India and Nepal, where he spent nine months studying Buddhism under Lama Yeshe. His life has been full of adventure, travel, and different jobs, including teaching English classes in Tokyo, construction work in Los Angeles, and mining in South Dakota and Colorado.

Ronald has a BA in political science from the University of Washington, as well as certificates in memoir writing and teaching English as a second language. He has been to every continent with the exception of Antarctica. Currently, he lives in Seattle, where he's a member of Hugo House and the Seattle Writers Meetup Group and taken advanced writing classes from Theo Pauline Nestor and Peter Mountford.